MAX notes®

Emily Brontë's

Wuthering Heights

Text by
Lynda Rich Spiegel
(M.A., Queens College)
Department of English
Brandeis School
Lawrence, NY

Illustrations by
Karen Pica

Research & Education Association

What **MAXnotes®** *Will Do for You*

This book is intended to help you absorb the essential contents and features of Emily Brontë's *Wuthering Heights* and to help you gain a thorough understanding of the work. The book has been designed to do this more quickly and effectively than any other study guide.

For best results, this **MAXnotes** book should be used as a companion to the actual work, not instead of it. The interaction between the two will greatly benefit you.

To help you in your studies, this book presents the most up-to-date interpretations of every section of the actual work, followed by questions and fully explained answers that will enable you to analyze the material critically. The questions also will help you to test your understanding of the work and will prepare you for discussions and exams.

Meaningful illustrations are included to further enhance your understanding and enjoyment of the literary work. The illustrations are designed to place you into the mood and spirit of the work's settings.

The **MAXnotes** also include summaries, character lists, explanations of plot, and section-by-section analyses. A biography of the author and discussion of the work's historical context will help you put this literary piece into the proper perspective of what is taking place.

The use of this study guide will save you the hours of preparation time that would ordinarily be required to arrive at a complete grasp of this work of literature. You will be well prepared for classroom discussions, homework, and exams. The guidelines that are included for writing papers and reports on various topics will prepare you for any added work which may be assigned.

The **MAXnotes** will take your grades "to the max."

Dr. Max Fogiel
Program Director

Contents

Each Chapter includes List of Characters, Summary, Analysis, Study Questions and Answers, and Suggested Essay Topics.

Introduction

The Life and Work of Emily Brontë

Emily Brontë, born in Thornton, Yorkshire, in northern England in 1818, is considered by *Nineteenth Century Literature* as a fascinating enigma. Living most of her brief life in the morally circumspect atmosphere of her father's parsonage in Haworth, Yorkshire, she failed, according to *Nineteenth Century Literature* to establish social contacts aside from her family. Yet, she was able to create in *Wuthering Heights* a world rife with tempestuous, passionate, vengeful characters. How, one wonders, was she able to depict violent human nature, given the seeming uneventfulness of her life?

Despite her reclusive nature, she was a great observer of life. Although she has generally been depicted as a recluse, she was, in fact, exposed to a cross-section of society through her father's congregation and their very diverse life experiences. In fact, the Yorkshire temperament has often been characterized as somewhat passionate and vengeful, replete with blunt manners and colorful speech. Clearly, Brontë had personal experience with the type of people she characterized in *Wuthering Heights*.

Her first exposure to the type of emotional cruelty depicted in *Wuthering Heights* may have come during her stay at the Haworth school. Educated there with her sisters, Emily could not help being aware of the special torment meted out to her sister Maria by the despotic headmistress. Indeed, even her life at home was not immune from life's seamier side. Her brother Branwell was a dissolute figure, addicted to both alcohol and drugs. Living amidst the sometimes rough Yorkshire gentlemen farmers of her father's parish, Brontë was undoubtedly exposed to the darker side of human behavior. Nevertheless, the extreme violence and obsessive passion in her art fascinates her readers for its sharp contrast with the conventional aspects of her life.

A seemingly insignificant event in her childhood fostered Brontë's creative imagination. When she was eight, her father bought his children a set of wooden toy soldiers. While playing with them, Brontë and her siblings Charlotte, Branwell, and Anne created imaginary lands about which they invented stories and poems, peopled with characters of their fancies. Emily invented an imaginary Pacific island called Gondal, which was the wellspring of her many romantic fantasies.

Although Brontë left her home briefly to study in Brussels, the death of the aunt who had raised her and her siblings forced her to return home at the age of 24 where she lived for the remainder of her life. While tending to household duties, she wrote poetry based on her childhood Gondal fantasies. Acting on Charlotte's suggestion, she published some of her poems with those of her sisters', using the pseudonym "Ellis Bell." Although the book, *Poems by Currer, Ellis, and Acton Bell* only sold two copies, the poems written by Emily were singled out by one critic as the best in the collection. Meanwhile, Brontë had been working on *Wuthering Heights*, which was published in 1847 together with her sister Anne's novel, *Agnes Grey*, and which followed on the heels of Charlotte's masterpiece, *Jane Eyre*. *Agnes Grey* fell into obscurity, while *Jane Eyre* met with critical acclaim.

Some Victorian critics, such as the one writing in the July 1848 issue of *Graham's Magazine*, objected to the "vulgar depravity and unnatural horrors" depicted in *Wuthering Heights*, asking how "a human being could have written such a book... without attempting suicide." In 1850, while working with the editors on the Second Edition of the novel, Charlotte defended *Wuthering Heights*, replete with authentic Yorkshire dialect and manners, as "realistic," although she allowed that it did contain sinister overtones. Her contemporaries were not quite ready for Brontë's sinister form of realism which fell far outside the mainstream of conventional Victorian sensibilities.

In any event, Brontë was not to live long after *Wuthering Heights* publication. She tended her brother, Branwell, while he was dying from alcoholism and drug abuse. During his funeral she caught a severe cold which developed into tuberculosis. Refusing medical attention, she died very shortly after him in December 1848.

Historical Background

The Victorian Age was a time of great economic, social, and political change. The British Empire had reached its height and extended throughout one quarter of the world. The beginning of the Industrial Revolution, it was a time of great prosperity for some, but abject poverty for factory and farm workers. Many Victorian writers dealt with the contrast between the prosperity of the middle and upper classes and the wretched condition of the poor. Indeed, class distinctions will appear as an important subtext in *Wuthering Heights*.

Like her fellow Victorian novelist, Thomas Hardy, Brontë's setting is limited to the Yorkshire moors of northern England, a rural, isolated region. Rural life was governed by a strict societal hierarchy which Brontë accurately depicted in *Wuthering Heights*. At the top were the Lords, the aristocracy, with its hereditary or monarch granted titles, large estates, political dominance and patronage system. Next came the gentry class, non-titled nobility landowners, who constituted local leadership. The Linton family in *Wuthering Heights* is typical of this class. Next were the gentlemen farmers, many of whom were prosperous enough to maintain a lifestyle like that of the gentry. Mr. Earnshaw, father of Hindley and Cathy, is a representative gentleman farmer. Indeed, the distinction between the two classes appears in the novel, when Catherine refers to herself and Heathcliff as being of "the lower orders" (Pool 160-166).

Wuthering Heights is unlike any other novel in the genre of Victorian literature in that it stands outside the social conventions of its time. Victorian literature characteristically viewed the individual as a member of society. In *Wuthering Heights*, Brontë for the first time portrayed society from a completely individual point of view.

While many of the great Victorian novelists of the early to middle period, such as Dickens, Thackeray, and Eliot, dealt more explicitly with moral preoccupations and social concerns than Brontë did, *Wuthering Heights* was unique for containing more of the primitive and spiritual side of the human spirit, feelings which, according to Derek Traversi, were "otherwise unduly concealed in this period."

Wuthering Heights, furthermore, with its mysterious, isolated mansions located in the wind-swept, brooding Yorkshire moors, is replete with overtones of Gothic horror. There is the suggestion of ghosts revisiting the living, supernatural allusions, and above all, a protagonist who symbolizes the dark side of mankind. These Gothic characteristics are more typical of the Romantic period of literature than the Victorian.

In fact, one could safely say that Brontë manages to anticipate the twentieth century novel. With its ambivalent morality, violence, and emphasis on the evil side of human nature, *Wuthering Heights* has much in common with modern novels, such as *The Sound and the Fury*. Indeed, Hindley Earnshaw's profligate behavior is reminiscent of Jason Compson's, as are the vicious intra-family feuds, and frustrated sexual urges.

Perhaps this is why the novel met with unfavorable critical reaction when it was first published. The general sentiment among critics was that the characters and their situations were too "disagreeable and coarse to be attractive." Charlotte Brontë was among the novel's chief admirers, although even she was forced to acknowledge how strange and wild *Wuthering Heights* must seem to those unacquainted with Yorkshire. More recently, writers such as Charles Percy Sanger and Virginia Woolf have described it as a novel of genius for the manner in which Brontë contrasts the civilized, genteel side of human nature with its wild, untamed counterpart. *Scribner's Companion* and Richard Benvenuto have also been impressed with Brontë's accuracy and consistency in detail. The characters age in accordance with correct sequence and behave in an age-appropriate manner. Brontë's depiction of the Yorkshire moors is accurate, as is her ear for the local dialect. Furthermore, she exhibits considerable knowledge of English inheritance laws in her handling of the characters' legal matters.

However much Brontë was disparaged by her contemporaries, twentieth-century critics rank her among the elite of Victorian writers for the genius she exhibits in *Wuthering Heights*. Ironically, her sister Charlotte, who received acclaim by those who objected to Emily, is now considered the less gifted writer.

Master List of Characters

Heathcliff—*The protagonist of the novel; an orphan raised at Wuthering Heights by Mr. Earnshaw, he soon dominates the fates of the Earnshaw and Linton families; a person of extremes, he is capable of passionate love for Catherine Earnshaw despite devoting his life to cruelty and revenge for his enemies.*

Catherine Earnshaw—*Daughter of Mr. and Mrs. Earnshaw, sister of Hindley, wife of Edgar Linton, mother of Cathy; a wild, tempestuous girl, she fails to thrive in the ordered and conventional world of the Lintons. She is the only person whom Heathcliff loves.*

Mr. Earnshaw—*The master of Wuthering Heights and father of Hindley and Catherine. He notices an orphan in a Liverpool slum and, naming him Heathcliff after a son who died in infancy, brings him to Yorkshire to be raised with his own children.*

Mrs. Earnshaw—*A minor character, she objects to her husband bringing Heathcliff into their home.*

Hareton Earnshaw—*An unkempt young man, Lockwood at first mistakes him for Heathcliff's son, but notes that he is treated like a servant.*

Hindley Earnshaw—*A disappointment to his father, Hindley is jealous of his father's affection for Heathcliff, fostering a lifelong hatred between the two; husband of Frances and father of Hareton.*

Frances Earnshaw—*The wife whom Hindley meets at college; she dies soon after giving birth to their son, Hareton.*

Mr. and Mrs. Linton—*Master and mistress, respectively, of the elegant Thrushcross Grange, parents of Edgar and Isabella; they* *invite Catherine to convalesce in their home, only to become ill themselves and die.*

Edgar Linton—*Master of Thrushcross Grange upon the death of his parents, he is, as a child, somewhat weak and spoiled. As he reaches adulthood, he becomes a respected member of society; a kind, gentle man, he dotes on his sister, Isabella and adores his wife, Catherine, and daughter, Cathy.*

Isabella Linton—*Sister of Edgar and mother of Linton Heathcliff, she is a foolish and overindulged girl. Her silly romantic nature leads her to fall in love with Heathcliff despite his obvious unsuitability.*

Catherine Linton Heathcliff (Cathy)—*Daughter of Catherine Earnshaw and Edgar Linton, she is gentle, like her father and headstrong, like her mother. She marries her cousin, Linton Heathcliff.*

Linton Heathcliff—*Son of Heathcliff and Isabella Linton, a sickly and effeminate young man; whining and self-pitying like his mother, with his father's bad temper.*

Mr. Lockwood—*Narrator of the novel and Heathcliff's tenant at Thrushcross Grange, his function is actually to allow Ellen Dean to narrate most of the past action to him while he convalesces from an illness.*

Ellen Dean (Nelly)—*Works for the Earnshaws as a young girl; she grows up with their children, serving Catherine and later Heathcliff. It is she who narrates most of the story to Lockwood. Since all the characters confide in her, she is the only character who is aware of all that goes on.*

Joseph—*An elderly servant at Wuthering Heights, he is self-righteous and pious; he speaks in a Yorkshire dialect that is sometimes difficult to follow.*

Zillah—*The housekeeper at Wuthering Heights while Nelly is at Thrushcross Grange caring for Lockwood.*

Mr. Kenneth—*The local doctor.*

Mr. Green—*A lawyer.*

Summary of the Novel

The first three chapters of the novel are narrated by Mr. Lockwood as a recollection from his diary several years after the events took place in 1801. Lockwood, a native of London, rents Thrushcross Grange, in the desolate Yorkshire moors, in order to enjoy some solitude. On a visit to his landlord Heathcliff's residence, Wuthering Heights, he encounters some unusually unhappy people: Cathy, Heathcliff's daughter-in-law, whom Lockwood at first mistakes for his wife; Hareton Earnshaw, an ill-bred young man whose social status leaves Lockwood confused; Joseph, the snarling, rude servant; and Zillah, the only helpful person there. Most forbidding is Heathcliff himself, a man whom Lockwood describes as even more unsociable than he.

Due to a raging snowstorm on his subsequent visit, Lockwood is forced to spend the night. While sleeping, he dreams of a ghostly child, identifying herself as Catherine Linton, grabbing at his arm and trying to get in through a broken window pane. Heathcliff is devastated to hear the dream and orders Lockwood downstairs so he can beg for the spirit to reappear.

Relieved to get away from this unhappy, strange house, Lockwood returns to the Grange. His housekeeper, Nelly, takes over from him as the narrator, due to his prodding about the inhabitants of the Heights. Her narrative returns to her childhood, some thirty years earlier, when she was a servant at the Heights. She was working for the Earnshaw family, and growing up with their two children, Hindley and Catherine, a beautiful, but wild spirited girl.

One day, Mr. Earnshaw had returned from a trip to Liverpool with a swarthy street orphan, who he intended to raise with his own children, against the wishes of his family. The boy is named Heathcliff, after a son who had died in infancy. Catherine and Heathcliff soon become close friends, but Hindley views Heathcliff as a rival for his father's affections. Indeed, Mr. Earnshaw does prefer Heathcliff to his own son, whom he views as a disappointment. Hindley's treatment of Heathcliff causes sufficient household friction that Hindley is sent away to college. Soon after, Mr. Earnshaw dies.

Hindley returns home for the funeral with a wife, Frances, upon whom he dotes. Redoubling his hatred for Heathcliff, Hindley relegates him to servile status, causing Catherine much unhappiness. She and Heathcliff are frequently punished, but escape to play on the moors.

During one such escape, the two venture to Thrushcross Grange, home of the Linton family and their children, Edgar and Isabella. Catherine, attacked by one of the dogs, is affectionately cared for, while Heathcliff is turned away for appearing to be a villain. When Catherine returns home after a five-week convalescence, she has become a well-mannered young lady. Taking pleasure in humiliating Heathcliff, Hindley tells him to come greet Catherine as if he were one of the servants. Later, when Edgar and Isabella come to visit, Hindley treats Heathcliff with particular humiliation. Heathcliff swears revenge on Hindley, even if it takes a lifetime.

Frances dies giving birth to a son, Hareton. Anguished, Hindley soon becomes lost in alcoholic madness. Meanwhile, Catherine tells Nelly that she will marry Edgar because Heathcliff is socially beneath her. Overhearing, Heathcliff runs away before Catherine admits how profoundly she loves him.

Three years later, Edgar and Catherine marry. Heathcliff returns, moving in with Hindley in order to gain his revenge by inducing him to gamble away all his money. A frequent visitor to the Lintons, Edgar soon becomes jealous of his wife's attachment to Heathcliff, and orders him to leave. Heathcliff gets his revenge on Edgar by eloping with Edgar's sister, Isabella. Although he despises her, Heathcliff marries Isabella in order to inherit her money. Catherine becomes dangerously ill, and dies after giving birth to a daughter, Cathy.

Treated contemptibly by Heathcliff, Isabella runs away to the South, where she gives birth to a sickly son, Linton. Upon her death, Edgar tries to keep Linton, but Heathcliff demands custody. Raising his daughter to avoid Wuthering Heights and its inhabitants, Cathy forgets about Linton until she sees him by accident some years later.

Heathcliff's revenge against the Earnshaw and Linton families includes garnering all their property for himself. He already possesses the Earnshaw estate, leaving Hareton an illiterate farmworker, completely dependent on Heathcliff. Heathcliff plans to do the same to Cathy, by forcing her to marry Linton, who cannot live past his teens, and therefore control all her inheritance as well.

It is now 1802, and Nelly has brought Lockwood up to date with her history. The story continues. Heathcliff succeeds in accomplishing his plans. Edgar and Linton are dead, and Cathy is as penniless and dependent as Hareton. When the two cousins fall in love, Heathcliff realizes he is no longer interested in destroying anything. He becomes obsessed with a vision of his beloved Catherine's spirit hovering nearby, waiting for him to join her. Within three days of his vision, Heathcliff dies and is buried according to his wishes, alongside Catherine. Local legend claims that their spirits haunt the moors.

Hareton and Cathy plan to marry on New Year's Day, moving back to Thrushcross Grange, and taking Nelly with them. Lockwood returns to London.

Estimated Reading Time

This is a lengthy book. Unless the reader is accustomed to the style of a Victorian novel, he or she may have difficulty understanding the language. Furthermore, Brontë occasionally has her characters speak in phonetic Yorkshire dialect. Therefore, an inexperienced reader will have to read slowly and carefully. The entire book can be read over a period of forty hours, less if the reader has some familiarity with nineteenth century literature.

Wuthering Heights

Chapter 1

New Characters:

Mr. Lockwood: *the first-person narrator of the story; tenant of Heathcliff*

Heathcliff: *the protagonist of the novel; a fascinating, yet surly and unpleasant man*

Joseph: *an elderly servant of Heathcliff who speaks with a thick Yorkshire dialect*

Zillah: *the housekeeper; the young woman's name is not disclosed until later in the book*

Summary

The story begins in 1801, as Lockwood, a new tenant in Thrushcross Grange, narrates the story of his visit to his new landlord, Heathcliff. Although Lockwood, a native of London, describes himself as a reserved man in search of a quiet place to live, he is surprised to learn that the beautiful, yet ruggedly isolated Yorkshire moors are inhabited by someone even more antisocial than he; Heathcliff is clearly reluctant to allow Lockwood inside his gate. When Heathcliff finally allows him in, Lockwood meets the servant Joseph, who is equally inhospitable.

We learn that Heathcliff's home is named Wuthering Heights. Wuthering is Yorkshire dialect for stormy weather. Indeed, there is

a powerful north wind which blows continually over the place and has permanently bent the surrounding trees.

Walking through the house, Lockwood offers a detailed description of the entryway, the kitchen, and parlor. Yet Lockwood is most intrigued by the contrast between the furnishings and the man who lives there. While the house itself seems normal enough for "a homely, northern farmer," Heathcliff himself is a study in contrasts. He looks like a dark-skinned gypsy, yet dresses and speaks like a member of the landed gentry. Lockwood attempts to rationalize Heathcliff's unfriendliness by identifying it with his own aversion to emotional attachments. He describes himself as being difficult to love or be loved, and gives an example of how he recently led a young woman into thinking he was interested in her, only to coldly withdraw, and thus earning himself a reputation for being heartless.

The two men sit, and to cover the awkward silence, Lockwood attempts to pet one of Heathcliff's dogs. The dog growls and Heathcliff says the dog is not a pet. He then calls for Joseph, who does not appear. After Heathcliff goes to look for Joseph, Lockwood winks and makes faces at the dogs. When one of the vicious animals attacks Lockwood, an unnamed young woman rushes to his aid, while Heathcliff merely praises the dog for its vigilance. Finally offering him some wine, Heathcliff excuses his lack of hospitality by saying he rarely has visitors. Heathcliff relaxes into a discussion of Lockwood's new home, proving to be a sufficiently intelligent companion, which leads Lockwood to conclude that Heathcliff doesn't want to antagonize his new tenant further.

On leaving, Lockwood offers to visit again the next day. Despite Heathcliff's lack of enthusiasm, Lockwood decides he will return.

Analysis

Although Lockwood, an apparently ordinary man, is an essentially minor character, he sets up a contrast between himself and the protagonist so that it is clear to the reader that there is something unusual, almost sinister, about Heathcliff. His behavior is extreme; the reader cannot understand why he delights in confusing Lockwood with his deliberately misanthropic behavior.

We are meant to understand that Heathcliff treats everyone in the same manner he has shown Lockwood. The reader is motivated to continue reading by the expectation of learning why Heathcliff is so antisocial, and what has happened to make him this way. We are also curious about the young woman who comes to Lockwood's aid. What is she, the only humane person Lockwood has met there, doing in such a place? The reader is grateful for Lockwood's insistence on returning the following day so that these mysteries can be solved.

Study Questions

1. How does Lockwood describe the Yorkshire section of England?

2. What makes Lockwood enter the gate, despite Heathcliff's rudeness?

3. Whose name does Lockwood see carved into the threshold, and why can't he ask about it?

4. What does Lockwood's instinct tell him about Heathcliff's reserved manner?

5. Why does Heathcliff leave Lockwood alone with his dogs?

6. What does Lockwood do to cause the dog to attack him?

7. How do Joseph and Heathcliff react to Lockwood's cry for help?

8. What reasons does Lockwood give for deciding not to make a further issue about his attack?

9. What final impression does Heathcliff have of Lockwood?

10. Does Lockwood give a reason for wanting to visit again?

Answers

1. Lockwood describes Yorkshire as a beautiful country, completely isolated, and "a perfect misanthropist's heaven."

2. Lockwood was interested in a man who was even less friendly than himself.

3. Lockwood sees the name Hareton Earnshaw, but can't ask about it because of Heathcliff's impatience.

4. Heathcliff's reserve believes Lockwood is a result of an aversion to showy displays of feeling.

5. Heathcliff has gone to find Joseph, who has not responded to his call.

6. Lockwood winked and made faces at the dogs, which caused one of them to break into a fury and attack.

7. Joseph and Heathcliff make no effort to come to Lockwood's aid.

8. Lockwood sees it would be foolish to sulk just because of some dogs, but mainly, he does not want Heathcliff to be amused by him being upset.

9. Lockwood sees that Heathcliff is very intelligent.

10. No. Lockwood merely says that he will return despite Heathcliff's obvious reluctance. Lockwood is clearly fascinated by a man less sociable than he.

Suggested Essay Topics

1. Compare and contrast the characters Heathcliff and Lockwood. Does Lockwood's impression of Heathcliff change by the time he leaves Wuthering Heights?

2. Discuss the meaning of the name of Heathcliff's home, Wuthering Heights. Does the name reflect on Heathcliff's personality or the home itself?

Chapter 2

New Characters:

Catherine Linton Heathcliff (Cathy): *after Lockwood mistakes her for Heathcliff's wife, he learns that she is his dead son's widow*

Hareton Earnshaw: *an unkempt young man, Lockwood at first mistakes him for Heathcliff's son, but notes that he is treated like a servant*

Summary

Due to bad weather, Lockwood thinks he might stay home rather than return to Wuthering Heights. However, one of the servants has begun making a mess cleaning out the fireplace, so Lockwood hastily departs for the four mile walk to the Heights, just as snow begins to fall.

Chilled by the freezing wind, Lockwood finds the door barred and curses Heathcliff's "churlish inhospitality." Nevertheless, he pounds on the door until Joseph overhears him from the barn and tells him no one is home but "the missus," and she won't open the door for anyone. As the snow begins to fall heavily, a young man signals Lockwood to follow him, leading him into the kitchen. There he sees a beautiful, slender young woman with long golden hair and a desperate look of unhappiness. She eyes Lockwood with scorn, refusing to invite him to be seated, and mocking him for mistaking a pile of dead rabbits for her pet lap dogs. Lockwood is rebuffed both in his attempt to help her get an out-of-reach object in the kitchen and in his request to be asked to stay for tea. The young man responds to his efforts with a glare that implies "some mortal feud unavenged" between them.

This uncomfortable atmosphere is exacerbated by Heathcliff's arrival. When Lockwood cheerfully speculates that he will have to remain at the Heights for half an hour before he can attempt the walk home, he is warned of the grave danger of being lost in the blinding snows of the Yorkshire moors. Lockwood asks for the loan of a servant to guide him, but Heathcliff rejects his request.

Tea is served by the young woman, and Lockwood is taken aback by the intensity of Heathcliff's obvious dislike for her. Feeling responsible for the gloomy mood his presence has caused, Lockwood foolishly attempts a conversation about the happiness of family life, referring to the young woman as Heathcliff's wife. He is told that Mrs. Heathcliff is dead, and then realizes his error was obvious; Heathcliff is near forty, while this young woman is seventeen. Lockwood regretfully concludes that the loutish young man is, in fact, her husband, and he determines that he will try to gain her affections himself.

Sensing Lockwood's confusion, Heathcliff tells him that the young woman is his widowed daughter-in-law. Asking the identity of the young man, Heathcliff tells Lockwood that he is "assuredly" not his son, leaving it to the young man to announce his name, Hareton Earnshaw, with a warning for Lockwood to show him respect. While the combined hostility from all three occupants of the Heights leads Lockwood to resolve never to return again, the intensifying storm necessitates his remaining for the night.

Joseph enters the kitchen, castigating the young widow, Cathy, by warning her she is heading to hell, like her mother before her. With what Lockwood interprets as a hidden sense of humor, she pretends to put a witch's spell on Joseph, causing him to flee. Encouraged by her humorous treatment of the old man, Lockwood appeals to her for help in getting home, but she says there is nothing she can do.

Heathcliff tells him he has no place for visitors; Lockwood must share a bed with Joseph or Hareton if he stays. Lockwood offers to sleep on a chair in the kitchen, but Heathcliff won't allow him to be unsupervised. Angered by this final insult, Lockwood pushes past Hareton to get outdoors. There he overhears Hareton offer to escort him part of the way, but Heathcliff refuses, saying Hareton must attend to the horses. When Cathy argues that human life is more important, Heathcliff once again turns on her viciously. This time, Cathy snaps back at him.

Borrowing a lantern, Lockwood begins to head home, only to have Joseph set the dogs on him for stealing it. Hareton and Heathcliff laugh as the dogs knock him flat, but Zillah again comes to Lockwood's aid and pulls him to safety. She gives him brandy, and shows him to a bedroom.

Analysis

This chapter offers further insight into Lockwood's character: he relies on conventional behavior to see him through the highly unconventional events at the Heights. Despite the hostility between Heathcliff and Cathy, Lockwood uses flowery Victorian language in assuming they are husband and wife. Additionally, we are reminded of Lockwood's alleged reputation for romantic heartlessness when he mentions his intention in trying to woo Cathy away from Hareton.

In this chapter we learn much about the lives of the residents of the Heights. We discover that Heathcliff was once married to a woman he ironically refers to as a "ministering angel." Further, we learn that his son is dead, and for some reason he holds the young widow in extreme contempt. Cathy, we discover, is not only beautiful, but has a temper. She has cleverly learned how to handle Joseph, and is not too afraid of Heathcliff to rebuke him occasionally.

Hareton is the most enigmatic character in the chapter. Although we finally learn the name of this disheveled, awkward young man, we still do not know who he is; Heathcliff orders him about like a servant, but unlike a servant, he sits at the table with Heathcliff and Cathy. Brontë continues to intrigue us with the information she continues to withhold. We sense that the relationships among these characters stem from a previous generation and look to future chapters for a clue to the hostility rampant among the residents of Wuthering Heights.

Study Questions

1. Why does Lockwood decide to return to the Heights?

2. Who lets Lockwood into the house?

3. How does Lockwood make himself look foolish to the young woman in the kitchen?

4. How does Lockwood respond when she asks him if he has been invited to stay for tea?

5. Who does Lockwood at first assume the young lady to be?

6. What does Lockwood intend to do when he incorrectly assumes she is married to Hareton?

7. Who unexpectedly tries to accompany Lockwood home?

8. How is Cathy related to Heathcliff?

9. What causes Lockwood to run out of the house?

10. Who comes to Lockwood's aid when he is again attacked by the dogs?

Answers

1. Despite the chilly weather, Lockwood wishes to escape the disruption of his servant girl cleaning.

2. Hareton beckons to Lockwood from the yard and leads him into the kitchen.

3. Lockwood mistakes a pile of dead rabbits for her pet dog, causing her to sneer, "a strange choice of favorites."

4. He tells her that she is the proper person to have issued the invitation.

5. Lockwood assumes the young lady is Heathcliff's wife.

6. He intends to make her regret choosing Hareton for a husband by making her fall in love with him.

7. Hareton unexpectedly offers to escort Lockwood part of the way home.

8. Cathy is Heathcliff's daughter-in-law, although her husband is dead.

9. Insulted by Heathcliff's insistence that he be under supervision while at the Heights, Lockwood runs outside, grabs a lantern, and tries to leave.

10. As she did in Chapter 1, Zillah rescues Lockwood.

Suggested Essay Topics

1. Discuss Lockwood's use of flowery Victorian language in assuming Heathcliff and Cathy are husband and wife. Why do you feel he would choose such language?

2. Discuss Lockwood's plan to woo Cathy away from Hareton. Argue whether or not Lockwood has genuine feelings for Cathy.

Chapter 3

Summary

Zillah leads Lockwood upstairs, cautioning him to keep quiet because Heathcliff doesn't allow anyone to use the room she is taking him to. Lacking a bed, Lockwood curls up in a hidden closet by a window, where he discovers a pile of books bearing the names Catherine Earnshaw, Catherine Heathcliff, and Catherine Linton.

Falling asleep for a few minutes, Lockwood awakens to the smell of his candle scorching the cover of a diary, inscribed with Catherine Earnshaw's name and dated twenty-five years ago. He reads what Catherine has written with increasing interest.

Catherine complains about her brother Hindley, who has become a tyrant since becoming master of the Heights after their father's death. While Hindley and his wife Frances cuddle in the warm parlor, Joseph forces Catherine and Heathcliff, shivering in the garret, to endure a three-hour sermon on religious texts. Catherine, followed by Heathcliff, finally rebels. In a fury, Joseph sends for Hindley, who scolds them, calling Heathcliff a vagabond, and threatens to evict him if he continues to act like a family member or play with Catherine again. Bringing Catherine to tears, Hindley blames their late father for having spoiled Heathcliff, and vows to "reduce him to his right place."

Overwhelming exhaustion prevents Lockwood from continuing to read Catherine's diary. He drifts into a dream in which Joseph accuses him of an unnamed crime and tells him he must repent before he will be allowed to return to Thrushcross Grange. Dreaming he is being attacked, Lockwood awakens to the sound of a tree branch brushing against the window.

Falling asleep for a second time, Lockwood has an even more terrifying nightmare. Hearing a tapping at the locked window, he breaks the glass in order to snap off the offending tree branch. Instead, he touches the ice cold hand of a sobbing child. The ghostly child tells him she is Catherine Linton, and begs to be allowed inside. Terrified by his inability to shake off the child's clinging hand, Lockwood drags her arm across the jagged glass, horrified by the blood which now drips across the bed. Breaking free at last, Lockwood barricades the broken window and screams, as the voice

continues to wail, "...twenty years. I have been a waif for twenty years."

His screams bring Heathcliff, who curses Lockwood's presence and threatens to harm Zillah for having brought him to this particular room. When Lockwood informs Heathcliff that a sinful ghost named either Catherine Linton or Earnshaw had tried to enter, Heathcliff becomes incensed. Ordering Lockwood to the kitchen until dawn, when he can safely return home, Heathcliff throws himself, sobbing, at the window ledge. As he descends the stairs, Lockwood overhears Heathcliff begging, "Cathy, do come in! My heart's darling! Hear me this time, Catherine, at last."

As the household awakens, Lockwood is again impressed with the misery of its occupants. Hareton rebuffs him, Zillah is shaken by Heathcliff's fury, and Cathy narrowly escapes being beaten when she defies Heathcliff. Lockwood leaves as soon as possible, arriving at the Grange weakened and chilled. The chapter ends as he gratefully submits to the care of his servants, who were worried when he failed to return.

Analysis

This chapter offers the reader a different view of Heathcliff. First, through Catherine's diary, we see the bitter resentment from Hindley Earnshaw that Heathcliff had to endure as a child. For the first time in the novel we can view Heathcliff with some sympathy. Secondly, as he sobs with great longing for Catherine, we see that he is capable of more than vicious hostility; this is a man who is capable of deep love. The reader may now sense that Heathcliff's misanthropic tendencies stem from his treatment at Hindley's hands, as well as from the loss of Catherine.

The supernatural element in this chapter (Catherine's ghost seems all too real to have been a dream) brings a Gothic mystery flavor to Wuthering Heights. That, together with Brontë's descriptions of the violent Yorkshire weather and the bizarre behavior of the characters (other than Zillah and Lockwood), contribute to the overall tension thus far in the novel.

Study Questions

1. What does Lockwood discover on the window ledge?

2. What is described in Catherine's diary?

3. How does Catherine view Hindley and his wife?

4. What torments Lockwood during his first dream?

5. What wakens Lockwood from this dream?

6. Who begs to be allowed into the room?

7. How does Lockwood get free from the child's grasp?

8. How many years has the child's ghost been wandering?

9. What is Heathcliff's reaction to Lockwood's screams?

10. Why does Heathcliff raise his hand to Cathy?

Answers

1. Lockwood discovers a few mildewed books piled in a corner.

2. Catherine describes a dreary Sunday afternoon in which she and Heathcliff are forced to endure Joseph's religious sermons.

3. Catherine thinks Hindley and his wife Frances are selfish, foolish lovebirds, negligent in their care of she and Heathcliff.

4. Lockwood is tormented by Joseph, who threatens him for his sins, and leads an attack on Lockwood.

5. A dry fir tree branch, brushing against the window, awakens Lockwood.

6. A ghostly child, calling herself Catherine Linton, begs Lockwood to let her enter.

7. He tricks her into letting go by telling her he cannot let her in if she doesn't let go.

8. The ghost says she has been a wandering waif for twenty years.

9. Heathcliff curses Lockwood for being in the room, threatens Zillah for taking Lockwood there, and, when alone, tearfully begs Catherine to enter.

10. Heathcliff is infuriated by the sight of Cathy sitting idly reading instead of earning her keep. When she refuses to work, he raises his hand to hit her, but she jumps away.

Suggested Essay Topics

1. Although Lockwood is a minor character, Brontë provides sufficient information for us to develop a clear picture of him. Write a brief character sketch describing Lockwood, focusing on his perceived similarities to Heathcliff.

2. In many novels, the setting functions like a character; without its unique qualities, the story wouldn't be the same. Describe the Yorkshire countryside, giving reasons why its characteristics are essential to the novel.

Chapters 4–5

New Character:

Ellen Dean (Nelly): *Lockwood's housekeeper, who has known all the characters for most of their lives*

Summary

Bored and in low spirits from being alone in his room, and recuperating from the frightful events at the Heights, Lockwood asks Nelly Dean to sit with him while he dines. Having developed a genuine curiosity about the residents at Wuthering Heights, he hopes she can offer some insights about them. As he had hoped, Nelly is an accurate historian; she provides him with several significant pieces of information. We learn that Heathcliff is quite wealthy, but tight-fisted; rather than enjoy the comforts of the Grange, he rents it out and lives in the relative decay of the Heights. Furthermore, Nelly tells Lockwood that Cathy is the daughter of Catherine and Edgar Linton, and that Hareton is Hindley's son, and thus Cathy's first cousin. Nelly's most important revelation is that she knows all about Heathcliff's past, except for where he was born, who his parents were, and how he first acquired his money. We also

learn that Heathcliff has somehow cheated Hareton of his inheritance. The novel continues at this point with Nelly as its narrator.

Nelly tells of Heathcliff's introduction to Wuthering Heights many years ago when they were children. Mr. Earnshaw left for Liverpool after promising to bring Hindley and Catherine gifts upon his return. Three days later he returned with a dirty, tattered orphan child, who, he told his wife, had to be taken "as a gift of God." The family is appalled. Despite Mr. Earnshaw's kindhearted refusal to leave the orphan starving on the streets, his wife scolds him, and his children, torment the boy for having crushed the gifts their father brought them. The children and Nelly refuse to allow the boy to sleep with them, and after spending his first night on the floor outside Mr. Earnshaw's room, he becomes a marginal part of the family. He is given the name Heathcliff after a son who had died in infancy.

Quickly, Catherine and Heathcliff become friends, but Hindley develops a chronic hatred for him. Nelly admits she hated him as well, and that he was barely tolerated by Mrs. Earnshaw. Although Heathcliff is tormented and unloved by nearly everyone, Mr. Earnshaw dotes on him, creating a source of intense jealousy in Hindley. Taking advantage of Earnshaw's affections, Heathcliff blackmails Hindley into giving him his horse by threatening to complain of Hindley's abusive behavior. Hindley complies, but beats Heathcliff further. Nelly is initially impressed with how stoically Heathcliff endures abuse, giving her the false impression that Heathcliff does not have a vindictive nature. She is proven wrong.

Mrs. Earnshaw dies. When Mr. Earnshaw's health fails, he becomes increasingly angered by his family's hatred for Heathcliff, and becomes more protective of the boy. The kinder members of the household, in an effort to please the dying Mr. Earnshaw, begin to spoil Heathcliff. This only exacerbates Heathcliff's cunning manipulations and bad temper. Relations between Hindley and Heathcliff become unbearable, especially since Hindley is aware that his father prefers Heathcliff over him. At the local curate's suggestion, Hindley is sent away to college.

As Earnshaw's health weakens, he allows Joseph, whom Nelly describes as "the wearisomest self-righteous pharissee that ever ransacked a Bible," considerable influence. Joseph's strict religious demeanor sways Earnshaw to reject Hindley completely for being a reprobate, and Catherine for being high spirited and mischievous. Indeed, he tells her that he cannot love her when she is bad. Snuggling close to her father, she seeks his forgiveness, but it is too late. Mr. Earnshaw dies peacefully in his home, leaving Heathcliff and Catherine to cling to each other for comfort.

Analysis

The reader begins to locate the source of Heathcliff's hostility in the rejection he suffered during his childhood. Even his lack of a surname served to place him in the lowest of social classes, a fact which later motivates him to become wealthy.

Perhaps the roots of his evil nature are psychologically embedded in the cruelty he suffered as an orphan on the streets of Liverpool and at the hands of Hindley. However, he doesn't seem to benefit from the positive influences, such as Earnshaw's devotion, or Nelly's efforts in caring for him. The love he and Catherine share, which initially seems to be based in a sibling-like attachment, is potentially the only positive influence on his developing into a "good" person.

Another interesting psychological study could be made from Hindley's situation. His father's insensitivity in rejecting him in favor of the orphaned Heathcliff is a cruel and permanent blow. Although we have little insight into Hindley's character before Heathcliff's arrival, Catherine's diary in Chapter 3 informs us that he is now a domineering tyrant.

Only Catherine, passionate, but mischievous, seems unaltered by her family situation. The reader will discover, in future chapters, the thing that will alter her high-spirited nature.

Study Questions

1. Why does Heathcliff live at the Heights instead of the Grange?

2. How is Cathy related to Hareton?

3. Who are the last remaining members of the Earnshaw and Linton families, respectively?

4. Under what circumstances did Heathcliff arrive at the Heights?

5. How did Heathcliff get his name?

6. What was the cause of Hindley's alienation from his father?

7. What sort of relationship did Heathcliff have with Hindley?

8. Where is Hindley when his father dies?

9. How does Catherine generally behave?

10. How do Catherine and Heathcliff react to Earnshaw's death?

Answers

1. Although the Grange is a nicer home, Heathcliff prefers to rent it out and live in the Heights.

2. Cathy and Hareton are first cousins; Cathy's mother, Catherine, and Hareton's father, Hindley, were siblings.

3. Hareton is the last remaining member of the Earnshaw family, and Cathy is the last remaining Linton.

4. Heathcliff was found, orphaned and starving, on the streets of Liverpool by Mr. Earnshaw, and brought home to be raised as a member of the family.

5. He was named Heathcliff, after a son who had died in infancy.

6. Due to Earnshaw's preference for Heathcliff, Hindley began to regard his father as an oppressor rather than a friend.

7. Heathcliff and Hindley hated one another; Hindley would physically torment Heathcliff, while Heathcliff used manipulative methods to antagonize Hindley.

8. Hindley is away at college when his father dies, mostly because their relationship is so difficult.

9. Catherine loves to tease her family and servants, yet is affectionate. She is considered too poorly behaved by her father to be his favorite.

10. Catherine and Heathcliff comfort each other in a touching and innocent scene observed by Nelly.

Suggested Essay Topics

1. Discuss the difference between the way Mr. Earnshaw treats Hindley and Heathcliff. Based on your reading of the novel, argue whether or not Mr. Earnshaw has any legitimate reason(s) why he treats Heathcliff better than Hindley.

2. Discuss the relationship between Catherine and Heathcliff.

Chapters 6–7

New Characters:

Frances Earnshaw: *Hindley's wife, who he introduces to the family at his father's funeral*

Mr. and Mrs. Linton: *neighbors at Thrushcross Grange, the adjoining estate*

Edgar Linton: *their son, a handsome, yet babyish mama's boy*

Isabella Linton: *their daughter, a spoiled and foolish girl*

Summary

Hindley arrives home for his father's funeral with his wife Frances, a silly, pretty girl with no apparent family connections. Hindley is reminded of his loathing for Heathcliff, and drives him from the family into the servants' quarters. Smitten with his wife, Hindley neglects Catherine's upbringing until Nelly fears she will grow up a savage. Under pressure from Joseph and the curate, Hindley allows Catherine and Heathcliff to be disciplined with church attendance and frequent punishments. They react to these measures by escaping to the moors where they can play. Under these conditions, Catherine and Heathcliff grow increasingly close and emotionally dependent upon each other.

On one such escapade, they venture to the Linton home, Thrushcross Grange. Spying on the family through the window, Catherine is attacked on the ankle by their dog. When she is carried inside, young Edgar Linton recognizes her as a Sunday school classmate, but Heathcliff is called a villain, deemed "quite unfit for a decent house," due to his cursing and his swarthy appearance.

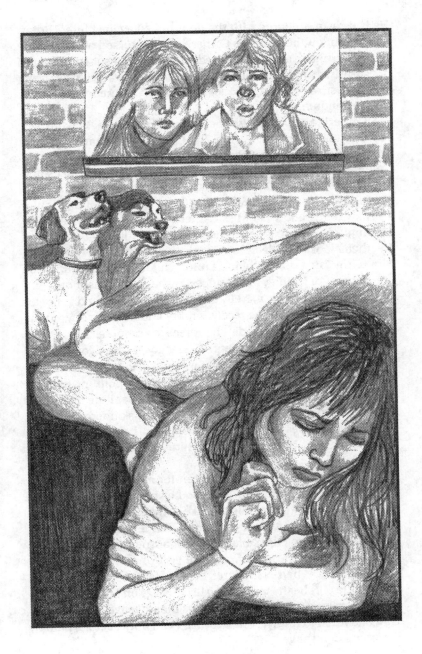

He is thrown outdoors with the door bolted against him. Hiding by the window, he observes Catherine being fussed over and petted as her injured ankle is attended to. Obviously insulted, although not surprised, by the Linton's treatment of him, Heathcliff tells Nelly that Catherine is far superior in her spirited nature to the insipid Linton children.

Catherine remains with the Lintons for five weeks while she recuperates. During that time, the Linton's well-mannered and conventional home life influences her behavior and she returns home a mirror image of Isabella Linton, much to Frances and Hindley's delight, and Heathcliff's disgust. Greeting her upon arrival, Hindley takes pleasure in humiliating Heathcliff by telling him he "may come and wish Miss Catherine welcome, like the other servants." Catherine is concerned to see how filthy and neglected Heathcliff looks, but decides that this is because she is comparing him to the fair-skinned, blond Linton children. Heathcliff, to the amusement of Hindley and Frances, rushes out of the room.

Alone in the kitchen, Nelly begins to feel sorrow and guilty for Heathcliff's situation. She resolves to try and help the boy, but he ignores her. The following day, he agrees to accept her help, for he wants her to make him "decent;" he is "going to be good." Nelly promises to groom him so that he will look handsome compared to Edgar Linton, and tries to encourage him by pointing out that Edgar is older, but Heathcliff is stronger. This does little to comfort Heathcliff, since he knows he can never be fair skinned or rich like Edgar. Nelly advises him that "a good heart will help him to a bonny face," and cheers him into believing himself a mysteriously handsome, dark prince.

The arrival of the Linton children for a visit quickly puts an end to Heathcliff's resolve to feel good by behaving well. Goaded by Hindley's refusal to let him partake of the refreshments, he immediately strikes out at Edgar Linton. Rather than accuse him, Catherine turns on Edgar, blaming him for speaking to Heathcliff. Hindley banishes Heathcliff, and the visit proceeds without further incident. When Nelly later brings Heathcliff down to the kitchen, he tells her he is planning his revenge on Hindley, regardless of how long it takes. Nelly advises him to leave vengeance to God and learn to forgive, but Heathcliff can only bear his pain by dreaming of revenge.

Nelly interrupts her narration here to apologize to Lockwood for talking so long. Assuring her he is quite enthralled with her story, he begs her to continue and leave nothing out.

Analysis

Chapter Six defines the polar worlds represented by Wuthering Heights and Thrushcross Grange. The Grange and its inhabitants, the Lintons, symbolize conventional Victorian society, that is, everything that is "good" and rational in human relations. The Heights, on the other hand, like the Earnshaws themselves, embodies everything that is evil and dysfunctional in humanity. Significantly, within moments of her arrival at the Grange, the effects of civilized behavior can be seen in Catherine. Heathcliff, as a reject from this bastion of conventional propriety, appears to be doomed to remain on the fringes of society, an untouchable outcast.

Yet, it is this rejection from society, combined with the reader's revulsion toward Hindley for his treatment of Heathcliff, that causes us to feel some sympathy for him. Even though we are immediately repelled by Heathcliff in the first chapters, in Chapter Seven we are moved to pity the ill-treated boy, particularly when be begs Nelly to help him be decent and good.

Further, Chapters Six and Seven set up the theme of revenge which dominates the entire novel. The earlier vision of Hareton, Hindley's son, as a servile illiterate deprived of his inheritance, now appears to mirror Hindley's treatment of Heathcliff. Heathcliff's behavior in the first chapters, seemingly inexplicable, can now be viewed as a part of the elaborate scheme for revenge he plotted in Chapter Seven.

Study Questions

1. What surprise does Hindley bring when he returns home?
2. What is Nelly's opinion of Frances?
3. What stern measures does Hindley impose on Heathcliff?
4. What circumstances cause Catherine to remain at the Grange?

5. How do the Lintons treat Heathcliff?

6. How has Catherine changed during her stay at the Grange?

7. When does Nelly begin to feel guilty about Heathcliff?

8. What does Heathcliff want Nelly to help him do?

9. What advice does Nelly give Heathcliff?

10. What causes Heathcliff to swear everlasting revenge on Hindley?

Answers

1. Hindley returns home with a wife, much to everyone's surprise.

2. Nelly thinks Frances is foolish, although she finds her thin, young, and fresh complexioned. Although she mentions that Frances has a troublesome cough, Nelly doesn't worry or sympathize.

3. Hindley no longer allows Heathcliff to eat or live with the family. He is sent to live in with the servants and work among them.

4. Spying on the Linton children, Catherine is bitten on the ankle by their dog, and is invited to recuperate at their home.

5. The Lintons treat Heathcliff as if he were a thief, and throw him out of their house.

6. After five weeks with the Lintons, Catherine returns home with much improved manners, and dressed like a fashionable young lady.

7. Alone in the kitchen, reflecting on Christmas' past, Nelly begins to feel pity for Heathcliff, and resolves to try to help him.

8. Heathcliff wants Nelly to help him be decent and good.

9. Nelly advises Heathcliff that a cheerful disposition will improve his looks; she also tries to boost his self-esteem by suggesting he is better looking than he thinks.

10. The final insult for Heathcliff is having Hindley evict him in front of Edgar Linton. Unable to endure Hindley's abuse any more, Heathcliff vows lifelong revenge.

Suggested Essay Topics

1. There is enormous hatred between Hindley and Heathcliff. Both boys feel cheated of something the other has. Which one do you feel has the more legitimate complaint? Defend Heathcliff or Hindley based on whom you believe has the most justification.

2. Social class issues begin to surface in Chapters Six and Seven. Much of Heathcliff's social inferiority is due to his swarthy appearance and lack of family background. Discuss his treatment by the Lintons compared to their behavior toward Catherine in this context.

Chapter 8

New character:

Mr. Kenneth: *the local doctor*

Summary

It is now 1778. Nelly's work in the hayfield is interrupted by the news that Frances has just given birth to Hareton, although the doctor believes that Frances' chronic tuberculosis (foreshadowed by Nelly's mention of her coughing in Chapter Six will shortly kill her. Rushing back to the house so she can begin to care for the infant, Nelly finds both Hindley and Frances in desperate denial of Frances' condition. Despite her brave efforts, Frances soon dies, leaving Hindley disconsolate.

Sinking into depression and alcoholism, Hindley takes no interest in Hareton, other than to object when his cries disturb him. While Hindley's dissipation worsens, and his treatment of Heathcliff grows even crueler, Heathcliff takes a perverse pleasure in watching Hindley deteriorate. In fact, the entire household completely falls apart. All the servants, except for Nelly and Joseph,

leave; and no one, not even the curate, will visit. Catherine, however, has remained friendly with the Lintons and continues to visit
them. She begins to "adopt a double character", remaining unruly
and wild at home, but at the Lintons' home, she is a model young
lady. At fifteen, she is the most beautiful girl in the countryside,
and Edgar is smitten with her. Edgar prefers her to visit at the
Grange, rather than come to the Heights; Hindley's profligate reputation frightens him, and he remains disgusted by Catherine's
friendship with the socially unacceptable Heathcliff.

One afternoon when Hindley is away, Heathcliff ventures into
the parlor to see Catherine. He appears to Catherine, who now
holds different social standards, as unschooled and lacking in social graces. This makes her uncomfortable to see him and height-
ens her awareness of Edgar's suitability. When it becomes apparent
that Heathcliff has no intention of leaving, she finally admits that
she is expecting Edgar and suggests he leave to avoid Hindley's
punishment. Heathcliff complains that she has been neglecting
him for Edgar, showing her a calendar marked with the many eve-
nings she has spent with the Lintons. They exchange angry words,
and as he leaves, Edgar enters.

Ordered by Hindley to stay within earshot when Edgar visits,
Nelly remains in the room, dusting. When she refuses Catherine's
demand for her to leave, Catherine creates an outburst. Edgar is
appalled to see Catherine pinch Nelly, and then lie to him about it.
Then, at the height of her tantrum, Catherine hits baby Hareton
and then Edgar himself. Shocked to witness this unforeseen side
of her nature, Edgar begins to leave the room, with Nelly warning
him of his luck "to have a glimpse of her genuine disposition."

Edgar's resolution to leave lasts only as long as it takes him to
walk outdoors. Nelly again encourages him to avoid Catherine, a
"dreadfully wayword" girl, but she notes that Edgar is too besotted
with her to leave. He is doomed to love her, despite the differences
in their natures. He returns to Catherine's room and shuts the door.
When Nelly comes in later to tell them that Hindley has arrived,
she perceives that the quarrel has brought them closer.

News of Hindley's arrival has an urgent effect on everyone:
Edgar swiftly mounts his horse, Catherine takes to her room, and
Nelly, hiding baby Hareton, takes the bullets out of Hindley's gun.

Analysis

Despite her care in appearing a conventional gentlewoman while in the Lintons' company, Catherine's true nature is revealed to Edgar. Since he is a product of his social class, a typical gentry gentleman, he is repulsed by her outward display of emotion. However, he is irresistibly attracted to her; he is, in fact, as Nelly says, "doomed." The use of this term foreshadows Edgar's fate. Even if he can satisfy his love by marrying Catherine, he is doomed to unhappiness with her, for their natures make them unsuitable companions. Unable to be passionate, Edgar can only be loving and gentle, traits which are viewed by Catherine as weaknesses. And, notwithstanding the attractions of social convention, Catherine is unable to repress her passionate selfishness.

In this chapter, Brontë introduces her theme of the divided self: the conflict between natural instincts, as exemplified by Catherine, and social values, as portrayed by Edgar. Both are at once attracted and repelled by the other, a combination that, while inevitable, will prove disastrous.

Study Questions

1. What is Mr. Kenneth's diagnosis of Frances' condition?
2. Who will care for Hareton once Frances dies?
3. How does Hindley react to Frances' death?
4. What happens to the household?
5. What is Nelly's opinion of Catherine's attitude?
6. How does Catherine maintain "a double character"?
7. At the age of sixteen, how does Heathcliff appear?
8. What is Heathcliff's complaint when he visits Catherine?
9. What does Catherine do to drive Edgar away?
10. What advice does Nelly give Edgar?

Answers

1. Mr. Kenneth believes that tuberculosis will have killed Frances before winter.

2. Hareton will be entirely under Nelly's supervision.

3. Hindley becomes despondent. He mainly gets drunk and returns home in wild and unpredictable moods.

4. All the servants except for Nelly and Joseph leave. No one, not even the curate, comes to visit anymore.

5. Nelly finds Catherine unbearably haughty, arrogant, and overly impressed with her own beauty.

6. Catherine maintains a "double character" by remaining headstrong at home, but lady-like at the Lintons.

7. Heathcliff has completely lost any self-esteem he might have had under Mr. Earnshaw's protection. Unschooled and morose, he seems to encourage aversion rather than friend-liness.

8. Heathcliff complains that Catherine spends all her time with the Lintons instead of with him.

9. Catherine has a peevish tantrum during which she pinches Nelly, lies about it, and hits Hareton and Edgar, as well.

10. Nelly advises Edgar to leave once he has discovered Catherine's true nature.

Suggested Essay Topics

1. Discuss Catherine's "double character." How does this affect her relationship with Heathcliff?

2. Discuss the theme of the divided self: Man's natural instincts in conflict with society's adopted values. Using Edgar and Catherine as examples, discuss how these two aspects of human nature can or cannot be reconciled.

Chapter 9

Summary

Little Hareton, terrified of his father's rages, allows Nelly to hide him when Hindley makes his drunken entrance. Claiming to have already murdered Mr. Kenneth, Hindley threatens to kill Nelly as well. Clearly accustomed to dealing with Hindley's behavior, Nelly calmly eludes his knife. Hindley, however, grabs Hareton, and when he cannot calm the trembling child, he becomes enraged and dangles him, feet first, over the stair rail. Startled by Heathcliff's entrance, Hindley loses his grip and drops the baby. Without realizing what he is doing, Heathcliff holds out his arms and catches Hareton, saving him from death. Nelly notes the look of disappointment on Heathcliff's face; his unwitting heroism cost him the chance to get revenge on Hindley.

As Nelly rocks poor Hareton to sleep, Catherine enters to confide to her that Edgar has asked her to marry him. Before she will divulge her answer, she wants Nelly's opinion. Appalled with Catherine's earlier behavior, Nelly says Edgar is a fool to have asked her. Petulantly, Catherine admits that she accepted his proposal. Aware that Catherine's feelings for Edgar lack sincerity, Nelly states her opinion: Catherine "loves" Edgar because he is handsome, rich, and adores her; what further problem can there be? With uncharacteristic candor, Catherine admits that her heart and soul tell her she is doing wrong.

In truth, she concedes, she loves Heathcliff. However, since Hindley has reduced him to servile status, marrying him would degrade her as well. Therefore, she swears, "He will never know how I love him; not because he's handsome, but because he's more myself than I am."

Unaware that Heathcliff has been eavesdropping on their conversation, the two women are startled when this last admission causes him to run outdoors, Catherine is convinced that he did not overhear her. Nelly, however, warns Catherine that marrying Edgar means that she and Heathcliff will have lost their friendship forever. Catherine replies that Edgar must learn to tolerate Heathcliff for her sake, and that by marrying him, she can even help Heathcliff by using Edgar's money to remove him from Hindley's power. Nelly scoffs at this idea. Catherine, however, clings to the conviction that she can manipulate Edgar, since she and Heathcliff must remain inseparable: "Nelly, I am Heathcliff."

Heathcliff, however, does not return. In a raging thunderstorm, Catherine sends Joseph and Nelly to search for him, and when they

fail to locate him, she scours the moors herself. Dripping wet, she sits up all night waiting for him, becoming dangerously ill with fever. At old Mrs. Linton's insistence, she is brought to the Grange to convalesce. She recovers, but both of Edgar's parents become ill and die within days of each other.

Heathcliff still does not return. Three years after his parents' deaths, Edgar brings Catherine to the Grange as his wife. At Catherine's insistence, Nelly accompanies her, forcing her to leave Hareton behind.

Nelly breaks off her narrative here due to the late hour. Lockwood agrees to go to sleep now, and hear more another time.

Analysis

Many readers focus on Catherine's description in this chapter of her love for Heathcliff, since the depth of their feelings for each other is central to the novel. Indeed, Catherine notes the difference between the "ordinary" love a man and woman share, and the intense bond which unites her with Heathcliff. Her love for Edgar, she declares, is "like foilage in the woods: time will change it," while her love for Heathcliff is an "eternal rock," invisible, but essential to her existence. Her statement, "I am Heathcliff" clearly expresses her belief that they share a soul.

Nevertheless, Catherine is willing, for the sake of respectability, to degrade her true feelings and marry Edgar. The reader can interpret that Brontë's intention was to portray Catherine as a victim of her social class which would have made marriage to Heathcliff impossible, forcing her to choose the socially acceptable Edgar. In any event, her overwhelming selfishness will not permit her to make a clean break; she is determined to have both men. Although some readers sympathize with Catherine's dilemma, others find her destructive in the pursuit of her desire. She will inevitably destroy something in either or both men; Heathcliff has already run away, while her presence at the Grange has already cost Edgar his parents.

Study Questions

1. What are Hareton's feelings for his father?

2. Why does Hindley dangle Hareton over the stair rail?

3. Who saves Hareton?

4. Why is Heathcliff angry with himself?

5. Why does Catherine say she loves Edgar?

6. What fault does Nelly find with Catherine's answer?

7. What bothers Catherine about her decision to marry?

8. What causes Heathcliff to run away?

9. How does Catherine become ill?

10. Why must Nelly leave Hareton?

Answers

1. Hareton is terrified of his father, never knowing if he will be kissed or killed.

2. Hindley is angered that Hareton will not respond to his attempts to soothe him.

3. Heathcliff enters just as Hareton falls, and reflexively catches him.

4. If Hareton had died, Hindley's remorse would have killed him. By saving the baby, Heathcliff has lost the chance to enjoy Hindley's destruction.

5. Catherine loves Edgar because he is handsome, pleasant, young, rich, and adores her.

6. Nelly says Edgar's love has nothing to do with Catherine's decisions; she is marrying him for his money and his looks.

7. In her heart and soul, Catherine feels she is doing wrong.

8. Heathcliff overhears Catherine's admission that their souls are as one, and that she can only love him.

9. Catherine catches a fever while searching for Heathcliff in the rain.

10. When Catherine marries, she insists that Nelly accompany her. Edgar and Hindley both enforce Catherine's wish.

Suggested Essay Topics

1. Write a character sketch of Edgar Linton, delineating his growth from a prissy, indulged child of privilege into a gentleman of honor and respect.

2. Discuss Catherine's decision to marry Edgar. Why does she choose to marry Edgar when she is in love with Heathcliff? Discuss Nelly's reaction to her decision.

Chapter 10

Summary

Lockwood has been recuperating for four weeks, and Mr. Kenneth does not anticipate him being allowed outdoors until spring. Heathcliff has been to visit; so grateful is Lockwood for the diversion he decides not to mention Heathcliff's role in causing his illness.

The visit reminds Lockwood that Nelly still owes him the next installment of Heathcliff's story. He begs her to fill him in on how Heathcliff became educated and wealthy enough to have become a gentleman. Nelly cannot answer these questions, and asks to be permitted to continue the story in her own fashion.

Catherine is fond of Edgar and his sister, and since they extend themselves to please her, the marriage seems successful. One day, Heathcliff appears at the Grange after a three-year absence, eager to see Catherine. Edgar is displeased to see the genuine joy with which Catherine greets Heathcliff, but she admonishes him to be friendly for her sake. Edgar is polite, but makes it clear to Heathcliff that he is welcomed as a childhood servant, nothing more. Amused by Edgar's strict adherence to conventional behavior, and truly overwhelmed with her delight in seeing Heathcliff again, Catherine quarrels with Edgar once Heathcliff departs (to Nelly's astonishment) for Wuthering Heights.

Complaining to Nelly that Edgar and Isabella are spoiled children, Catherine rebuffs her response that it is she who is the spoiled child: their peaceful household is dependent on Edgar and Isabella indulging Catherine. Laughing, Catherine swears that Edgar loves her so much, even if she tried to kill him, he wouldn't try to retaliate. Nelly tartly suggests she learn to value her husband's adoration, instead of ridiculing him.

The talk turns to the surprising news that Heathcliff has taken up residence with Hindley, a sign to Nelly that Heathcliff is exhibiting a Christian show of forgiveness to his sworn enemy. However, Catherine informs her that Hindley has been losing money to Heathcliff while playing cards and his gambling debts have made him susceptible to Heathcliff's offer to pay him well in exchange for lodging in close proximity to the Grange. Furthermore, Hindley has borrowed money from Heathcliff by pledging the Heights as security for his debts. Therefore, Nelly's assumption is quite incorrect.

During Heathcliff's frequent visits, Isabella becomes irresistibly attracted to him. Edgar is horrified not only to think of his sister degrading herself with such a questionable man, but of the thought that Heathcliff might inherit the Linton property should he and Catherine not produce a male heir. Edgar is convinced that Heathcliff has embarked on a deliberate campaign to marry Isabella to secure his fortune.

Jealous of the attention Heathcliff pays Catherine, Isabella and she quarrel. Nelly advises Isabella to forget Heathcliff, "a bird of bad omen." Catherine humiliates Isabella by telling Heathcliff of her infatuation. Encouraged by the opportunity to inherit Edgar's fortune through marriage to Isabella (despite the fact that he holds her in great contempt), the chapter ends with Heathcliff mulling over his next move, and Nelly expressing her premonition that he is up to no good.

Analysis

The theme of revenge resurfaces in this chapter as Heathcliff considers the benefits of marrying Isabella. Doing so will cause Edgar anguish, for he knows Heathcliff doesn't love his sister; Catherine will be punished for marrying Edgar instead of him; and most importantly, the possibility of inheriting the Linton fortune will make him financially capable of ruining Hindley.

We also learn in this chapter how fragile the peaceful Linton household really is. Serenity is dependent on Edgar's willingness to accede to Catherine's wishes, a harmless enough situation until she demands Heathcliff's acceptance into their home. The reader is aware that Heathcliff's intentions are evil and self-serving. His newly acquired gentlemanly manners are as superficial as Catherine's ladylike behavior. Heathcliff's true nature mirrors Catherine's: they are both selfish and determined to get what they want.

Study Questions

1. Why is Lockwood so pleased when Heathcliff visits?
2. What information about Heathcliff does Lockwood wish to know?
3. What has Catherine's life been like at the Grange?
4. After how many years does Heathcliff return?
5. How does Catherine react to his return?
6. Why is Heathcliff living at Wuthering Heights?
7. Who becomes infatuated with Heathcliff?
8. Why does this cause Edgar distress?
9. How does Catherine react to Isabella's interest in Heathcliff?
10. How does Catherine embarrass Isabella?

Answers

1. Lockwood has been alone, recuperating for four weeks, and is desperate for company.
2. Lockwood does not know how Heathcliff became educated or how he got his money.
3. Life has been very pleasant. Catherine is fond of her husband and sister-in-law, both of whom indulge her every whim.
4. Heathcliff has returned after three years.
5. Catherine is overjoyed, and tells Edgar he must be friendly to Heathcliff for her sake.

6. Since Hindley owes large gambling debts, he cannot refuse the generous rent Heathcliff is willing to pay him.

7. Isabella Linton becomes strongly attracted to Heathcliff, despite the fact that he does little to hide his contempt for her.

8. Not only does he love his sister and worry that she will be hurt, but Edgar fears that through marriage, Heathcliff will inherit the Linton property.

9. Knowing that Isabella is no match for her in Heathcliff's affections, Catherine is more amused than jealous.

10. Catherine tells Heathcliff how Isabella longs for him.

Suggested Essay Topics

1. Discuss Heathcliff's plan for revenge. How does his plan affect Edgar, Catherine, Hindley and Isabella?

2. Discuss Isabella's attraction to Heathcliff. How do Edgar and Catherine react to Isabella's feelings for Heathcliff?

Chapters 11–12

Summary

While dwelling on Hindley's deterioration, Nelly comes across a stone on the highway which had been a favorite spot of theirs as children. There she sees a vision which convinces her of Hindley's impending death. Rushing to the Heights, she encounters Hareton. She is horrified to discover what has become of the little boy she once nursed. Heathcliff has taken him under his wing; he no longer studies with the curate, but has learned how to curse and hit. Nelly asks him to send for Hindley so she can speak with him. However when Heathcliff appears instead, she turns and runs.

When Heathcliff next visits at the Grange, Nelly observes him trying to kiss Isabella and reports this to Catherine, who quarrels with Heathcliff. Accused by him of jealousy, Catherine retorts that if Heathcliff sincerely likes Isabella, she will do everything she can to help him. Heathcliff assures her that if he wants to marry Isabella, he needs neither her help nor Edgar's consent.

Nelly hastens to inform Edgar of Catherine and Heathcliff's quarrel. Incensed at Heathcliff's presumptions, Edgar confronts him and orders him to leave. Clearly frightened of Heathcliff, Edgar endures Catherine's taunts about his cowardice until he finally strikes Heathcliff on the throat, stunning him. Heathcliff is maddened by Edgar's burst of courage and threatens to kill him. However, Edgar has gone for assistance, and Heathcliff escapes.

Undone at the thought of losing Heathcliff, Catherine assures Nelly she will harm herself as punishment to Edgar if he tries to prevent her from seeing Heathcliff. When Edgar demands that Catherine choose between Heathcliff and himself, Catherine demands to be left alone and stages what Nelly terms "a senseless, wicked rage." Edgar is frightened to see her gnash her teeth, draw blood, and then faint. Nelly tells him not to worry and exposes Catherine's earlier threat. Hearing this, Catherine locks herself in her room, refusing to eat.

Giving up on Catherine momentarily, Edgar cross-examines Isabella to determine how far Heathcliff's advances have gone. Angered by her evasiveness, Edgar warns her that he will never speak to her again if she encourages Heathcliff's attentions.

After three days of fasting, Catherine emerges from her room, claiming she will soon die. Nelly ignores her, believing this to be pure manipulation. Angered that Edgar is able to work while she is in anguish, Catherine's emotions escalate from "feverish bewilderment to madness." One moment she is violent, the next she babbles. Thinking she is being haunted by a vision of an old hag, she is startled to realize that it is her own reflection in the mirror which startles her so. Exhausted and subdued, she hallucinates about being a child at the Heights, reliving Hindley's enforced separation between her and Heathcliff.

Convinced at last that she has gone mad, Nelly tries to restrain her in bed. At this point Edgar comes in, and seeing that Catherine is genuinely delirious, threatens to fire Nelly for not having told him about his wife's condition. Hurrying out in pursuit of Mr. Kenneth, Nelly is aghast to see Isabella's pet dog hung by the neck from a tree, close to death. Kenneth arrives, and Nelly fills him in on

Catherine's condition, blaming it on "the Earnshaw's violent disposition." In turn, Kenneth advises her that Isabella was seen running off with Heathcliff the night before. Tying this in with the mystery of the nearly strangled dog, Nelly rushes to Isabella's room. Her suspicions are confirmed; the room is empty.

Edgar bears the news of Isabella's elopement stoically, saying that he has not disowned her, but she has disowned him. Instead, he devotes himself to Catherine, who, Kenneth hopes, will recover if she can be kept calm.

Analysis

Catherine's mad rage reminiscent of Hamlet's, leaves the reader wondering whether or not she has truly gone insane or is acting so for purely manipulative reasons. In any case, it underscores her mystical, almost holy conviction that she and Heathcliff are fatefully united. It is arguably the most dramatic scene in the novel, removing Catherine's connection to Heathcliff from any pretext of conventional friendship, and focusing instead on the passionate, primitive longing she has for him.

Meanwhile, Heathcliff's senseless brutality towards Isabella's dog anticipates the treatment she can expect from him once their elopement is complete. The very idea that he is willing to marry a girl who he hates in order to gain the Linton Estate, his eagerness to advance his schemes for revenge on Hindley, Edgar, and perhaps even Catherine, demonstrates the level of his bitterness.

Study Questions

1. What vision causes Nelly to rush to the Heights?
2. What does she discover about Hareton?
3. How does Catherine learn of Heathcliff's attentions to Isabella?
4. How does Catherine react?
5. When does Edgar confront Heathcliff and order him to leave?
6. Why does Edgar hit Heathcliff?
7. What demand does Edgar make of Catherine?

8. How does Catherine react to Edgar's order?

9. Why doesn't Nelly take Catherine's hysteria seriously?

10. What news does Kenneth bring of Isabella?

Answers

1. Nelly sees an omen of Hindley's impending death.

2. Under Heathcliff's direction, Hareton's education has been stopped, and instead he has learned to curse and hit.

3. Nelly observes Heathcliff trying to kiss Isabella, and tells Catherine.

4. Catherine accuses Heathcliff of insincerity.

5. When Nelly tells him Heathcliff and Catherine have been quarreling, Edgar orders him to leave.

6. Heathcliff tells Edgar he is not worth striking. Catherine calls him a coward, so Edgar hits Heathcliff.

7. Edgar demands Catherine choose between Heathcliff and himself.

8. Catherine tells Edgar to leave, locks herself in her room, and refuses to eat.

9. Nelly believes Catherine is being manipulative.

10. Isabella was seen running off with Heathcliff.

Suggested Essay Topics

1. Describe Hareton. How has Heathcliff influenced Hareton's behavior?

2. Based on your reading of the novel, argue whether Catherine has truly gone insane, or is she acting insane for purely manipulative reasons?

Chapters 13–14

Summary

Under Edgar's devoted care, Catherine slowly recovers her health, but remains weak and depressed. To Edgar's delight, Catherine is pregnant, and he is certain the baby will be a boy, thus eliminating Heathcliff's claim to the Linton fortune. Six weeks after Isabella's departure, she sends Edgar a letter which he ignores. The remainder of Chapter 13 is narrated by Isabella in the form of a subsequent letter to Nelly.

Isabella and Heathcliff have moved into the Heights. In her letter, Isabella expresses her horror at each of the inhabitants of Wuthering Heights, especially Heathcliff. She begs Nelly to let her know if Heathcliff "is a man? If so, is he mad? And if not, is he a devil?" Describing her arrival, Isabella complains that Heathcliff had deserted her in the kitchen, where Hareton curses her for trying to kiss him, and Joseph disgusts her by using his hand to stir their dinner. Hindley is a shadow of his former self, and warns her to lock her door, lest he accidentally shoot her for Heathcliff. There is no maid to wait on her, and even worse, no bedroom for her to occupy. When Joseph finally comprehends that she wishes to be shown to Heathcliff's room, she discovers that it is locked, forcing her to spend the night on a chair in Hareton's room.

Wretched, Isabella begs Nelly to secretly visit her, but Nelly goes at once to inform Edgar of his sister's condition. Edgar allows Nelly to visit her and extend his regrets, but refuses to write to Isabella himself.

Visiting Isabella, Nelly notices that she has sunken to the level of slovenliness customary at the Heights. Heathcliff ridicules her to Nelly, calling her a disgrace even to the Lintons. He justifies himself by saying that he never mislead Isabella into thinking he cared about her. In fact, no demonstration of his coarseness, even his attempt to strangle her dog, deterred her from running off with him. In fact, he claims to wonder why she fails to act on her threat to leave. Faced with Isabella's despair, Nelly asks her why she stays with a monster such as her husband. Isabella explains that in reality she is kept prisoner in order to completely break her spirit.

Bored with tormenting Isabella, Heathcliff asks Nelly for news of Catherine. He entreats Nelly to help him visit her, promising he will hide from Edgar. He knows how deeply Catherine loves him, and how little regard she has for Edgar. Isabella speaks up in defense of Edgar, but Heathcliff mocks her by pointing out Edgar's loss of regard for his wayward sister, and orders her out of the room.

Alone with Nelly, Heathcliff convinces her to take a letter to Catherine by insisting that Catherine must be in hell with no word from him for so long. He is certain that Catherine is not flourishing, but suffering under Edgar's insipid attentions. Nelly struggles with her conscience all the way home. She knows she did wrong by accepting Heathcliff's letter, but she believes that Catherine's mental state will improve once she hears from Heathcliff.

Nelly stops her narration when Kenneth arrives to visit Lockwood. Lockwood mulls over what he has heard, and wonders what would happen if he fell in love with Cathy, only to discover she was "a second edition of the mother!"

Analysis

Isabella's emotional and physical decline parallels Catherine's; neither of them can endure an environment which is foreign to her. Catherine's attempt to become a conventional, decorous gentlewoman means she must squelch her passionate nature. She wastes away even as she prepares to give birth to the next generation of Lintons. Soon after she removes herself from the civilized society of the Grange, Isabella's standards of gentility give way to Heathcliff's hypnotic influence.

It is clear that part of Heathcliff's revenge is to hold complete control over both Hareton and Isabella. By controlling their lives, he can cause their degradation and suffering in the same manner he endured from Hindley and Isabella's family. Meanwhile, Heathcliff continues to exhibit a dual personality; he is still passionate and loving to Catherine, but cold and manipulative of everyone else. The other characters elicit no sympathy from him, they are merely his pawns. Even Nelly, from whom he has known friendship, is treated as a conduit, a means of getting messages to and from Catherine.

Study Questions

1. Is Catherine's recuperation completed?
2. What gives Edgar further hopes for her recovery?
3. What does Isabella write to Edgar?
4. How does Isabella now regard her husband?
5. What impression does Isabella get of Hindley?
6. Why does Hindley warn Isabella to lock her bedroom door?
7. What does Nelly ask Edgar to do?
8. How does Isabella appear when Nelly visits her?
9. Why does Isabella tell Nelly she cannot return home?
10. What requests does Heathcliff make of Nelly?

Answers

1. No, while Catherine's return to physical health is coming slowly, her mental state is still weak.
2. Edgar is pleased that Catherine's pregnancy will produce an heir, thus removing the threat of Heathcliff's claim.
3. Isabella tells Edgar she is married to Heathcliff and apologizes for having offended him.
4. Isabella wonders if Heathcliff is insane or simply the devil.
5. Isabella barely recognizes Hindley; he is terribly thin and extremely slovenly, although his eyes were "like a ghostly Catherine, with all their beauty annihilated."
6. Hindley tells Isabella when he is drunk at night, he may be tempted to shoot Heathcliff, and would not wish to hit her by mistake.
7. Nelly hopes Edgar will write Isabella a note which she can deliver, but he refuses.
8. Isabella no longer appears to be a gentlewoman, and seems reduced to the level of slovenliness tolerated at the Heights.

9. Isabella tells Nelly that Heathcliff is keeping her a virtual prisoner.

10. Heathcliff wants information on Catherine's condition; he wants Nelly to arrange a secret visit, or at least to deliver his letter to her.

Suggested Essay Topics

1. Both Isabella and Catherine are literally "fish out of water" in the residences they married into. Discuss how each woman responds to an environment which is unnatural to her.

2. Heathcliff is certain that Catherine loves only him. Based on your reading of the novel, argue whether or not Catherine has legitimate feelings for her husband.

Chapters 15–16

Summary

One week has gone by, and Nelly finds the time to continue relating her story to Lockwood.

Four days after her visit to Isabella, Nelly has the opportunity while Edgar is in church to give Catherine Heathcliff's letter. She presses the letter into the apathetic woman's hand, but Catherine is too depressed to even notice it is from Heathcliff and does not react until he enters the room.

Catherine kisses Heathcliff, and he returns it with "more kisses than he ever gave in his life before." Looking into her face, he realizes that she is close to death, and, in anguish, they cling to each other with such intense passion that they make "a strange and fearful picture." Catherine accuses him of joining with Edgar in having broken her heart, and claims he will forget her after she dies to find happiness elsewhere. He is distraught at her words, and she asks his forgiveness.

Catherine tells Nelly not to feel sorrow for her impending death, rather to envy her, for she regards death as a release from her earthly prison. Heathcliff asks Catherine if she is possessed by the devil, to talk so sanguinely of her death. He begs her not to torture him after she dies, thus driving him as mad as she is now.

Suddenly, Nelly observes Edgar returning from church and implores Heathcliff to leave at once, but Catherine will not release him from her arms. Aware that she will soon die and it is the last time she will ever hold her beloved soul mate, she cries out that Edgar will not harm them. As Edgar approaches, resigns himself to the possibility of death, so that he and Catherine can be together. Catherine faints. Seeing them together, Edgar rushes to attack, but Heathcliff hands him Catherine's limp body and begs him to take care of her first before they speak. Heathcliff goes to the garden to wait.

At midnight, Catherine gives birth to her daughter, Cathy, and two hours later, she is dead. Nelly tries to think how to break the news to Heathcliff, but he already knows. Moved to pity, Nelly assures him that in death, Catherine appears to be at peace. Maddened, Heathcliff prays that Catherine's soul know no rest until he himself is dead. "Be with me always—" he begs. "—take any form —drive me mad! ...I cannot live without my soul."

Edgar sits with Catherine's coffin until the funeral, while Heathcliff holds vigil in the garden below. When Edgar leaves her side for a few hour's rest, Nelly beckons Heathcliff in to allow him to say goodbye. Heathcliff unclasps the locket she has around her neck, removes its contents (undoubtedly Edgar's hair), and replaces them with a lock of his own.

Hindley fails to appear at his sister's funeral, and Isabella is not invited. Catherine is not buried in the family vault, but on a lovely green hill by the moors. Nelly tells Lockwood that Edgar lies in the same spot now.

Analysis

The reader now understands Heathcliff's despair in Chapter Three that Lockwood, rather than he, discovered Catherine's ghost. We now realize that her spirit has obeyed his pleas to have no rest until he, too, is dead. Heathcliff's desire to be haunted by her is thwarted by knowing her ghost is searching for him and cannot find him.

We are also aware that one aspect of Heathcliff's revenge will now come true. Since Catherine and Edgar's baby is a girl, contemporary English inheritance laws allowed for the Linton property to pass to Isabella at the time of Edgar's death. This means that as her husband, Heathcliff will control Edgar's estate, a horrifying thought which will trouble Edgar for the remainder of his life.

Heathcliff's astonishing hostility for Cathy in the early chapters now begins to make some sense. Since Catherine died giving birth to the girl, it is likely that Heathcliff associates her existence with the loss of Catherine. We have yet to learn how Cathy came to be Heathcliff's daughter-in-law, since Heathcliff has no son, a mystery which future chapters will answer.

Study Questions

1. What does Catherine do with Heathcliff's letter?

2. What does Catherine accuse Heathcliff and Edgar of doing?

3. What about Heathcliff and Catherine's embrace disturbs Nelly?

4. Why won't Catherine let go of Heathcliff, even as Edgar approaches?

5. How does Edgar react when he sees Catherine in Heathcliff's arms?

6. When does Catherine finally die?

7. How do Edgar and Heathcliff mourn Catherine?

8. What does Heathcliff pray for when Catherine dies?

9. Who is absent from her funeral?

10. Where is she buried?

Answers

1. Catherine lets the letter drop from her hand without even noticing it is from Heathcliff.

2. She says they both have broken her heart, yet each of them pities himself, rather than her.

3. She feels that she is "not in the company of a creature of my own species."

4. Aware that she is dying, she wants to hold him one last time.

5. Edgar is furious, but Heathcliff hands her to him and tells him to take care of her first.

6. Around two o'clock in the morning, two hours after giving birth to her daughter, Cathy, Catherine dies.

7. Edgar holds vigil by Catherine's coffin while Heathcliff mourns down below in the garden.

8. Heathcliff wants Catherine's soul to know no rest until he can join her in death; until then, he begs her to haunt him, for he "can't be without his soul."

9. Neither Hindley nor Isabella attend the funeral.

10. Catherine is buried on a grassy hill near the moors.

Suggested Essay Topics

1. Describe Catherine's feelings towards her impending death.

2. Why does Heathcliff want Catherine's soul to know no rest until he is dead? Do you feel he is selfish?

Chapter 17

Summary

Immediately following Catherine's funeral, the pleasant weather becomes cold and dismally chilly, setting the tone for Edgar's grief, Cathy's motherless state, and Isabella's rebellion.

Sitting alone with baby Cathy, Nelly hears an intruder, and is amazed to discover Isabella, dripping wet, bruised, and exhausted. Isabella insists on having a carriage take her to town and a few of her former belongings packed before she will consent to let Nelly tend to her woebegone condition. Once Nelly does as she asks, Isabella sits by the fire to explain her escape, requesting that Nelly put the baby away; she "doesn't like to see it!"

Isabella flings her wedding ring into the fire, daring Heathcliff to search for her simply as a way to antagonize Edgar. Proudly, she refuses to ask Edgar for any help, since he has not been kind to her since her defection. Babbling and somewhat hysterical, she utters her regret that Hindley is in no condition to kill Heathcliff for both their sakes; that, she says, would have been worth remaining behind to witness.

Indeed, Isabella claims, she should and wishes she could stay at the Grange to help Edgar raise Cathy, but knows Heathcliff would not allow her. Acknowledging that he detests her, Isabella knows that Heathcliff would rather endure her presence than allow her and Edgar to be content. Rid of her depressed desire to die at Heathcliff's hands, Isabella now only wishes he would kill himself, since he is a monster. She wonders how Catherine, knowing his true nature, could have loved him, and concludes that she must have had "an awfully perverted taste."

When Nelly protests that she should be more charitable to Heathcliff since he is a human being, Isabella flatly denies his humanity. The return of her instinct for self-preservation is due to her pleasure in learning how to antagonize him, and now that she is free, if she ever sees him again, she swears her revenge on him.

The narration switches here to Isabella, who regales Nelly with the events precipitating her escape. Hindley, too drunk to attend the funeral, sits in the kitchen with Isabella, taking advantage of Heathcliff's pre-funeral vigil at the Grange. When Heathcliff is heard outdoors, Hindley tells Isabella that if they were both not cowards, they should punish Heathcliff for what he has done to each of them, and thus end their misery. Isabella wants nothing more than to be free but objects to using treachery and violence, which "wound those who resort to them, worse than their enemies!" Hindley retorts that Heathcliff deserves to be treated with treacherous violence, since that is how he deals with everyone, and if she will allow him, he would turn it on the "hellish villain" himself.

As Hindley prepares to shoot, Isabella warns Heathcliff but he merely curses, while Hindley swears at her for interfering. Heathcliff warns Isabella to let him in, or he'll make her regret it, but she refuses, saying Hindley is waiting by the door with a gun and a knife. She advises him to go to Catherine's grave, and die alongside "the whole joy of your life!" At this, Heathcliff breaks through a window and disarms Hindley, catching the knife in Hindley's flesh. With his blood still dripping, Heathcliff pockets the knife and pounds Hindley's head into the stone floor, stopping only at Joseph's threat to send for Edgar, who is village magistrate.

In the morning, Isabella notices that Hindley was too drunk to recall the details of the previous evening's violence. Hindley sorrowfully wishes for the strength to kill Heathcliff, but Isabella says it is bad enough that Heathcliff has caused Catherine's death, and recalls how happy she and Catherine both were before he returned. Hearing her, Heathcliff sobs, and Isabella laughs at him. Attacking her with a knife, she dodges, and throws one back at him. Lunging for her, Hindley manages to block him, and so she escapes, knocking over Hareton, who is hanging a litter of puppies.

Having completed her tale, Isabella departs. Nelly resumes the narration, informing Lockwood that Isabella had moved near London and given birth to a son, Linton. Heathcliff doesn't follow her, but keeps himself apprised of his son from afar. When Linton is twelve, Isabella dies.

Meanwhile, Edgar avoids the sight of Heathcliff, and is gratified to learn that Isabella has left him. Although he still mourns his wife, he takes consolation in his young daughter, Cathy. Nelly compares Edgar's gracious reaction to adversity with Hindley's, pondering how the two men, both gentlemen by birth, deviated in their behavior. Despite Edgar's weakness as a boy, Nelly observes that he has matured into the stronger man.

Six months after Catherine's death, Mr. Kenneth arrives to tell Nelly of Hindley's demise. Nelly weeps for the loss of her childhood friend and pleads with Edgar to be allowed to organize his funeral. Furthermore, she reminds Edgar of his moral obligation to Hareton, who, as Catherine's nephew, has no other family. Edgar agrees to let Nelly bring Hareton to the Grange to live.

Discussing Hindley's affairs with his attorney, Nelly learns that Hareton is penniless. All of Hindley's estate has been heavily mortgaged to Heathcliff. He grudgingly permits her to give Hindley a decent burial at his expense, but surprises her by refusing to relinquish Hareton to Edgar's guardianship. Caressing the child roughly, he tells Nelly that raising a child might be amusing, and if Edgar

insists on taking Hareton, Heathcliff will take Linton away from Isabella. Halted by this threat, Edgar does not press further. As a result, Hareton, who by birthright ought to be the neighborhood squire, is completely dependent on his father's enemy—impoverished and friendless—and, most sadly, unaware of the injustice done him.

Analysis

This chapter is filled with harrowing details about domestic life at the Heights, even worse than what Lockwood experienced at the start of the novel. There seems to be no limit to the torture and degradation Heathcliff delights in heaping on Hindley and Isabella. Hindley is extraordinarily pathetic in his inebriated, futile attempts to kill Heathcliff, yet he touches Isabella with the suggestion of his former gentlemanly self when he speaks to her. Nowhere can we recognize the angrily authoritative young man he was, so thoroughly has Heathcliff orchestrated his ruin.

The change in Isabella is evident in this chapter. No longer a foolish romantic, Isabella has seen far too much to remain innocent. She rallies her internal strength. Rather than allow Heathcliff to ruin her as he has Hindley, she learns to fight back. It may be difficult to understand why she warns Heathcliff of Hindley's trap, since she knows his death will benefit everyone. We can interpret her refusal to engage in vengeance and treachery as a manifestation of her true nature; she was raised to be a Christian gentlewoman, not an avenger. Remaining true to her upbringing is a sign of her emotional recovery from her ordeal.

Study Questions

1. Why has Isabella returned to the Grange?
2. What plan did Hindley have for Heathcliff after the funeral?
3. Why does Isabella warn Heathcliff of Hindley's trap?
4. What prevents Heathcliff from beating Hindley to death?
5. How does Isabella finally get away from Heathcliff?
6. How does Nelly's response to Isabella's criticisms of Heathcliff show that her feelings toward him have mellowed?

7. Who has helped Edgar overcome his grief at losing his wife?

8. Where does Isabella go after her escape?

9. How does Hindley dies?

10. Why does Edgar decide not to fight Heathcliff regarding Hareton's custody?

Answers

1. Isabella has just escaped from the Heights, and needs Nelly to get her fresh clothes and a carriage to town.

2. Hindley schemes to free Isabella and himself from their misery by either shooting or stabbing Heathcliff to death.

3. Although she never says why directly, Isabella had earlier rejected using vengeance and treachery to free herself.

4. Joseph warns Heathcliff that he has gone too far, and he will summon the magistrate (Edgar) if Heathcliff doesn't stop.

5. Isabella goads Heathcliff to tears by mentioning Catherine's name. When she laughs at him, he throws a knife at her. Throwing it back, he lunges for her, but Hindley blocks him, and she escapes.

6. Nelly takes Isabella to task for her uncharitable remarks, rather than agreeing with them. This shows Catherine's death has altered her ill feelings for Heathcliff.

7. Edgar's baby daughter, Cathy, has completely won his heart.

8. Isabella moves near London, where she gives birth to Heathcliff's son, Linton, and dies twelve years later.

9. At the age of twenty-seven, Hindley dies of alcoholism.

10. He fears Heathcliff's threat to take Linton away from Isabella if Edgar takes Hareton to the Grange.

Suggested Essay Topics

1. Are Hindley and Isabella equally victims of Heathcliff's scheming, or did they in some manner "deserve" what happened to them at his hands? Using what you know about

both of their backgrounds, discuss to what extent Brontë intends us to pity them.

2. Both Isabella and Catherine are pregnant in these chapters, yet neither one even mentions it. What significance is there to their combined disinterest in motherhood? Referring to both Mrs. Earnshaw and Mrs. Linton, discuss how Catherine and Isabella were mothered, and locate a reason why maternity is not regarded as a joy for either of them.

Chapters 18–19

Summary

Following the tumultuous climatic events of Chapter 17, Nelly spends the next twelve years tranquilly raising Cathy. The child is a beauty, with her mother's dark eyes and her father's fair skin, delicate features, and golden hair. Like her mother, she is high-spirited, but lacking Catherine's wild nature. In her ability to form close attachments, she reminds Nelly of Catherine, but the child is gentle and thoughtful, like Edgar. Nelly does admit that Cathy is overindulged by Edgar and the servants, and so has a "propensity to be saucy" and perverse.

Living a reclusive life, studying at home with her father and restricted to Thrushcross Grange and its adjoining park, Cathy grows restless, begging to be permitted to visit Pennistone Crag, visible from her window. Since travel to Pennistone would involve passing Wuthering Heights, Nelly and Edgar evade giving permission.

Edgar receives word from Isabella that she is dying, and she wishes to make amends with her brother and deliver Linton to his care. Edgar leaves at once and is gone for three weeks.

During this time, Nelly tries to keep Cathy amused by creating imaginary adventures for her to enact while riding her pony on the estate. Nelly is confident that Cathy will not go beyond the estate gates, but when she fails to return one day for tea, the first place Nelly thinks to look for her is Pennistone Crag. Unable to reach Pennistone on foot before nightfall, Nelly stops at the Heights, only to discover that Cathy is there, chattering to Hareton. Nelly

chastises her for disobeying orders, telling her it is unsuitable for
her to be in this house. Cathy is surprised; she has mistaken
Hareton for the owner's son. Discovering she is in error, she assumes he is a servant, and orders him to get her pony. Embarrassed,
he curses, and when Cathy threatens to report him, Zillah reproves
her, telling her that Hareton is Cathy's own cousin. Confused, because Linton is the only cousin she has heard of, Cathy cries, leaving Nelly exasperated for having a well-kept family secret disclosed.

On the way home, Cathy tells Nelly that on the way to
Pennistone, her dog got into a fight with one of Heathcliff's, and
Hareton had come to her aide. Nelly extracts from her the promise
that Cathy will not tell Edgar where she has been, explaining that
he objects to "the whole household" at the Heights. She warns
Cathy that her father will be so angry, he will fire Nelly for her neg-
ligence. Cathy promises not to tell her father.

When Edgar arrives with Linton, Cathy is delighted to meet
her "real" cousin. She and Nelly both are unprepared for the spec-
tacle of Linton Heathcliff. He is unbearably peevish and sickly. On
the very night of his arrival, Joseph appears to remove Linton to
the Heights, under Heathcliff's orders. Edgar prevails on Joseph to
inform him of Isabella's request that Linton be raised at the Grange,
but Joseph is adamant. Firmly, Edgar refuses to send the boy that
night, telling him Heathcliff must wait until morning.

Analysis

In these chapters, the members of the next generation meet.
Immediately, Hareton is beguiled by Cathy. She convinces him to
guide her to the "fairy cave," and the shy, unsocial youth is riveted
by her chatter. The unintended insult of her assumption that he is
a servant momentarily brings his barbaric upbringing to the fore
as he curses at her. When she cries, he is repentant, and brings her
some puppies to play with. This contrasts with an earlier scene in
which Isabella trips over him as he is engaged in hanging puppies
by the neck. Cathy's effect on Hareton, as well as their future relationship, are foreshadowed by this event.

Cathy also meets the pale and unpleasant Linton. Although a
wretched character, Cathy treats him with the gentleness instilled
in her by Edgar. Pity, and not genuine love, seems to be the

motivating factor in her interest in him, since he does not seem hardy enough to make a good playmate. Her passionless pity serves to explain the relationship she develops with Linton in future chapters.

Linton is heartily disliked by Nelly and patiently tolerated by Edgar. Accustomed to having his wishes catered to, he is peevish and insensitive to others. Despite Cathy's attentions, he is not really interested in her at all and seems impervious to her beauty. Linton's self-absorption is so complete that he is aware only of himself. The reader is unsure how much of his sickliness is genuine, since he appears to be more coddled than ill.

In contrast, Hareton is a robustly healthy young man who, despite his social awkwardness, is sensitive to others. The reader recalls the kindness Hareton had shown to Lockwood, a virtual stranger. Certainly, he is prepared to dote on Cathy and is genuinely concerned when he sees he has upset her. Even Heathcliff and Joseph, the two curmudgeons, treat Hareton with affection.

Tension rebuilds in the novel, as the reader contemplates Linton's life with Heathcliff. We are also unsure about the direction Cathy's relationship with each of her cousins will take.

Study Questions

1. Why does Cathy want to visit Pennistone Crag?

2. Where does Nelly locate Cathy?

3. How did Cathy and Hareton meet?

4. For whom does Cathy mistake Hareton?

5. Why doesn't Cathy believe Hareton is her cousin?

6. What are some of Nelly's observations regarding Hareton?

7. How has Joseph treated Hareton?

8. How do the villagers speak of Heathcliff?

9. How does Linton arrive at the Grange?

10. Why does Edgar agree to let Linton go to his father the following morning?

Answers

1. Bored by her restrictions to Thrushcross Park, Cathy wants to explore beyond its boundaries.

2. Nelly finds Cathy sitting in the kitchen at the Heights.

3. As Cathy rode past the Heights, one of the dogs began fighting with Cathy's dog. Hareton came out to help, and agreed to escort Cathy to the Crag.

4. At first, Cathy assumes Hareton is the master's son, but then decides he must be a servant.

5. Cathy is unaware of Hareton's existence. The only cousin she knows of is Linton.

6. Nelly sees a good-looking, athletic eighteen-year-old dressed in farmer's clothes. She senses he is innately intelligent, and laments that Heathcliff has left him unschooled.

7. Joseph has not interfered with Heathcliff's neglect of the boy, but has instilled in him a pride in his name and background.

8. The villagers say Heathcliff is a cruel, hard landlord to his tenants, but that at least his unsociable behavior keeps the house free of the debauchery Hindley had caused.

9. Arriving in Edgar's coach, Linton is wrapped in a warm cloak, as if it was winter, and sleeps with fatigue from the trip.

10. As much as he regrets it, Edgar has no choice; Heathcliff insists, and he is within his rights.

Suggested Essay Topics

1. Describe Cathy. Do you feel she is more like Edgar or Catherine?

2. How do the other characters respond to the arrival of Linton?

Chapters 20–21

Summary

Edgar warns Nelly not to let Cathy know that Linton will be living at the Heights; he fears she will insist on visiting him and thus meet Heathcliff.

Linton is perplexed as to why he has to move to the Heights, since he has never heard of his father, and asks Nelly why he has not seen him before. Nelly quickly invents a tale that Heathcliff was too busy to visit, and Isabella never mentioned him to Linton because she didn't want him to miss his father.

Heathcliff and Linton meet. Rudely, Heathcliff insults Isabella for not having told the boy he has a father. Linton is shocked at Heathcliff's manner. Nelly pleads with him to be kind to the boy, since he is all he has and is delicate. Laughing, Heathcliff says he will be very kind. He has ordered Hareton and all the servants to obey Linton's wishes. Despite Heathcliff's declaration that he despises the boy, he wants to fulfill his revenge; he will own the Grange on Edgar's death, as he already owns the Heights, and he wants the triumph of knowing his son will have Hindley's son working under him.

Meeting a servant one day in town, Nelly learns that Linton's hypochondria isolates him from the others in the house. The servant describes him as demanding and whining, rebuffing Hareton's good-natured attempts to amuse him.

Two years later, on her sixteenth birthday (never celebrated since it is also the anniversary of Catherine's death), Cathy entices Nelly to a hill not far from Wuthering Heights, where they encounter Heathcliff and Hareton. Heathcliff charmingly invites Cathy into the house to rest; Nelly protests, but Heathcliff prevails. His scheme is for Cathy and Linton to become reacquainted, fall in love, and marry. Should they marry, Nelly points out, Catherine would inherit Linton's money when he dies (since he is clearly too frail to live long). However Heathcliff informs her that she is wrong; Heathcliff will inherit his dead son's estate, giving him possession of Cathy's money and land. Nelly resolves never to allow Cathy the opportunity to visit at the Heights again.

Pleased to see Linton again, Cathy is surprised to learn that Heathcliff is her uncle by marriage. She asks why her father has never spoken of him, and Heathcliff tells her Edgar thought him unfit to wed his sister, and is insulted that Heathcliff won her over his objections.

To Heathcliff's disgust, Linton is too self-absorbed to converse with Cathy. She asks if it is indeed true that Hareton is her cousin. Heathcliff affirms this, and considers aloud how much pleasure he takes in having molded Hareton into the perfect instrument for his revenge. Since Hareton is intelligent, he suffers at the extent of his debasement, exactly as Heathcliff did in his youth. Furthermore, even though Linton is a weakling, he is Hareton's social superior; even though Hareton has first-rate qualities, "they are lost, rendered worse than unavailing." Best of all, Heathcliff gloats, Hareton, who should by rights hate him, loves Heathcliff. His revenge on Hindley is complete and satisfying.

The visit ends with Linton ridiculing Hareton for being illiterate. Hearing his social deficiencies enumerated to Cathy, Hareton retreats, mortified. Nelly and Cathy return home, Cathy indignant at her father for barring "Uncle" Heathcliff from her life.

The next day, Cathy confronts Edgar only to learn his side of the feud. He describes Heathcliff's brutish treatment of Isabella, and Cathy, unaccustomed to anything but her own gentle rearing, is profoundly shocked. Edgar ends the discussion, asking Cathy to consider what he has told her and avoid further contact with the residents of the Heights.

Drawn to Linton, however, Cathy defies her father and Nelly, and smuggles a letter to him. A secret correspondence between the two flourishes, until Nelly catches Cathy and confronts her. Hearing that Cathy imagines herself in love with Linton, Nelly threatens to show the letters to Edgar, unless Cathy consents to having them burned. Cathy is distraught, but Nelly is firm. A note is sent requesting that Linton cease writing to Cathy.

Analysis

The focal point of Chapter 21 is the delineation of Heathcliff's design for his revenge on Hindley. Everything has proceeded perfectly, according to plan, giving Heathcliff immense satisfaction at the exquisite symmetry of his design. He refers to Linton as "tin

polished to ape a service of silver," and to Hareton as "gold put to
the use of paving stones." He admits his revenge would be less
sweet if Hareton were not inherently so fine a man; thus is his debasement more than pity. Further, Heathcliff clearly empathizes
with the young man, remembering how he, too, suffered the in-
dignities he was forced to endure at Hindley's hands. Yet Heathcliff
feels no guilt at how he has used Hareton, instead channeling his
feelings for the boy into the sort of affection a master feels for his
loyal dog.

For Linton and Cathy, however, Heathcliff feels unmitigated
loathing. He views them as embodiments of everything he dislikes
about the Linton family. His son is in every way his antithesis: weak,
foolish, pale and sickly. In Cathy, he sees nothing of Catherine, viewing her kindness and innocence as weaknesses inherited from
Edgar.

Study Questions

1. Why does Nelly feel sorry for Linton when he leaves his
   uncle's house?

2. How do Joseph and Heathcliff react when they meet Linton?

3. What does Linton say to Nelly when she leaves?

4. How do Hareton and Linton get along?

5. What plan does Heathcliff have for Linton and Cathy?

6. Why does Cathy leave Wuthering Heights upset with Edgar?

7. How does Heathcliff embarrass Hareton?

8. How do Linton and Cathy develop their relationship?

9. What are Cathy's feeling for Linton?

10. How does Nelly put a stop to their correspondence.

Answers

1. Nelly feels bad that she has had to lie to the poor boy by telling him his visit to Heathcliff is only temporary.

2. They ridicule him. Joseph says he looks more like a girl than
   a boy, and Heathcliff says he appears to have been "reared
   on snails and sour milk."

3. Linton begs Nelly not to leave him at the Heights.

4. Whenever Hareton attempts to be friendly, Linton cries and exasperates him. Linton learns to scorn Hareton for his lack of gentility, and enjoys mocking him.

5. He wants them to marry. Aware that Linton is not expected to live long, Heathcliff can secure ownership of Cathy's inheritance if she is Linton's wife.

6. Heathcliff has led Cathy to believe that Edgar began the feud between them.

7. Heathcliff asks Cathy in Hareton's presence if she finds him attractive.

8. They initiate a secret correspondence, using the local milk delivery boy as their messenger.

9. She believes she is in love with him, although Nelly points out they have spent less than four hours in each others presence.

10. She threatens to tell Edgar, unless Cathy allows her to burn Linton's letters. Then she sends Linton a note telling him to stop writing.

Suggested Essay Topics

1. Compare Linton to Hareton, focusing on Heathcliff's analogy in Chapter 21 of them as tin to gold. Both young men are pawns in Heathcliff's schemes. Which is the more sympathetic character? Why?

2. Why is Cathy drawn to Linton? Do you believe she is genuinely in love with Linton?

Chapters 22–23

Summary

Bedridden with a bad cold, Edgar is unavailable to keep Cathy company. Feeling sorry for her, Nelly tries to spend more time with the girl. One day as they are out rambling, she learns that Cathy often cries at the thought of Edgar's death; without Edgar or Nelly, she will have no one. Nelly comforts her by saying Edgar's illness is not serious, and as for herself, she is very healthy. Relieved, Cathy clambers over a gate, only to find herself unable to climb back. While Nelly searches among her keys for one to open the lock, Heathcliff arrives on horseback.

Cathy refuses to speak to him in accordance with her father's wishes, but Heathcliff cajoles her into feeling guilty for having stopped corresponding with Linton. He assures her that Linton has fallen seriously ill due to her neglect, and charmingly begs her to visit Linton while he is away. Exasperated at Heathcliff's manipulations, Nelly smashes the lock, and drags Cathy home, protesting all the way that Heathcliff is lying and Linton is undoubtedly fine.

Cathy insists on checking on Linton for herself, and Nelly grudgingly accompanies her to the Heights. There they find Linton coughing and feverish, but in an extremely ill temper. Cathy fusses over him, but the visit soon degenerates into a quarrel in which they each accuse the other's parent of causing trouble. When Linton asserts that Cathy's mother loved his father, Cathy pushes him. He falls and coughs so violently that Cathy is truly contrite. He orders her to leave, but she begs to be allowed to stay, fussing over him until Nelly is compelled to call him "the worst-tempered bit of sickly slip that ever struggled into its teens!"

As they depart, Linton asks Cathy to return the next day, but Nelly firmly forbids it. Laughing, Cathy says she is not a prisoner, and that she intends to nurse Linton, who will undoubtedly outlive her. Nelly retorts that if Linton isn't likely to die from his illness, there is no need for Cathy to return. Nelly threatens to inform Edgar, silencing Cathy into a sulky silence.

The next morning, Nelly has come down with a cold. She is touched at how devotedly Cathy tends to both her and Edgar. Convinced that the girl has been dividing all her time between the two patients, Nelly does not realize that the glow on Cathy's cheeks comes from her ride across the moors at Wuthering Heights.

Analysis

Cathy's insistence in these chapters in getting her own way is reminiscent of Catherine's willfulness, although Cathy's is motivated by good intentions, not selfishness. Nelly is powerless to stop her from seeing Linton, and Edgar is unaware of what is going on during his confinement. The plot moves inexorably toward a union between the two cousins, which further fulfills Heathcliff's schemes.

Heathcliff, of course, is in complete control of the situation at this point in the novel. He is able to exploit Cathy's good nature by appealing to her on behalf of Linton, whose death he himself eagerly awaits in order to stake his claim on the Grange. Whether or not Edgar dies soon, Heathcliff in any event will own all or part of Edgar's estate.

Study Questions

1. Who does Cathy say she loves more than herself?

2. How does Cathy become Heathcliff's momentary captive audience?

3. Why does Heathcliff say Linton is dying?

4. Why does Nelly grudgingly permit Cathy to check on Linton?

5. About what do Cathy and Linton quarrel?

6. What makes Cathy feel guilty about the quarrel?

7. Why does Cathy feel compelled to return the next day?

8. Why is Edgar unaware of Cathy's visit to Linton?

9. How long does Nelly remain ill?

10. During that time, what has Cathy been doing?

Answers

1. Cathy loves her father more than anyone, even herself.

2. Cathy is temporarily stuck behind the locked door of a stone wall on the estate grounds. While Nelly tries to smash the lock, Cathy has no choice but to hear what Heathcliff has to say.

3. Heathcliff claims that grief and disappointment in Cathy's abandonment have made Linton deathly ill.

4. Nelly is confident that Cathy will find out that Heathcliff has been lying.

5. They call each other's father's liars, and Linton says Catherine hated Edgar and loved Heathcliff.

6. Angered, Cathy pushes Linton, who coughs alarmingly and calls her a "cruel, spiteful thing." Seeing him moaning in pain, she is moved to cry from guilt.

7. Cathy feels Linton would get better more quickly if she were looking after him.

8. Edgar assumed Cathy and Nelly had been out wandering in the park.

9. Nelly is bedridden for three weeks.

10. In between caring for Nelly and her father, Cathy has been slipping away to visit Linton.

Suggested Essay Topics

1. Describe Cathy's relationship with her father.

2. How is Cathy similar to her mother? How does she differ?

Chapter 24

Summary

Sensing something odd in Cathy's behavior, Nelly waits by a window and soon sees the girl returning home on horseback. Confronted, Cathy admits she has been visiting Linton while Nelly has been bedridden. Pleading for Nelly's understanding, Cathy narrates the events of the past three weeks at the Heights.

During the first visit, she and Linton argue about each one's favorite diversion, but compromise by agreeing to the merits of both sides. Cathy attempts to play games with Linton, but he becomes peevish when she wins consistently, yet allows her to calm him with her singing.

On the second visit, however, an unpleasant scene develops between Hareton, Cathy, and Linton. Greeting Cathy, Hareton eagerly demonstrates his first steps in learning to read. When Cathy notes that this is all he has accomplished, he responds with anger. Ignoring him, she goes in to visit Linton in the parlor, only to have Hareton burst in, throw them out of the room and bar the door. Linton throws a coughing fit, and as blood gushes from his mouth, Cathy seeks Zillah's assistance. Guilt-ridden, Hareton meanwhile carries Linton to his bed, calling over his shoulder for Cathy to go home. Joseph locks the sobbing girl out, but Zillah soon directs her back inside. Hareton clumsily attempts to apologize for what he has done, but Cathy, incensed, snaps her whip at him. She runs off as he curses at her.

Nervous about returning, she nevertheless does so, and learns from Zillah that Linton is mending nicely. However, he sulks at her arrival and refuses to speak to her for an entire hour. Finally, he snaps at her, laying the blame for the previous events on her, not Hareton. Unable to reply, she stalks out silently. Two days later she returns to settle matters between them. Linton admits he is a worthless young man; his father has often reminded him of this. However, he prevails upon Cathy to believe him as capable of goodness as she, and tells her he loves her. Accepting his apology, they reconcile. Cathy is further encouraged that her attentions to Linton are needed. On one subsequent visit, she overhears Heathcliff verbally abusing the boy.

Having told Nelly everything, Cathy asks her not to tell Edgar. Thinking it over, Nelly decides she must let him know. Edgar's alarm at this turn of events is profound. He vehemently forbids Cathy to return to the Heights again, relenting only to agree to write Linton, inviting him to visit Cathy at the Grange. Nelly notes that had Edgar been acquainted with Linton's unpleasant nature, he would not have permitted even that.

Analysis

Hareton's basic decency is demonstrated several times in this chapter, yet he is continually rebuffed by Cathy's insensitivity. Failing to realize that Hareton is the better of the two young men, she concentrates only on Linton, for whom she possesses a romantic interest based on his helplessness. When Nelly rebukes her for her unkind treatment of Hareton—after all, he is her cousin as well—Cathy calls him a brute. Brutish as he can often be, Hareton is capable of knowing when he has done wrong and is eager to make amends. The reader is moved to pity him for being usurped by the sickening Linton in Cathy's favors. To carry the pet dog motif mentioned in the Analysis of Chapters 20 and 21 further, the image we carry of him when Cathy cuts him with her whip is that of a scolded puppy.

Additionally, the reader should note the love triangles which are paralleled in both generations of the Earnshaw and Linton families. The Hareton-Cathy-Linton triangle repeats that of Heathcliff-Catherine-Edgar, but with a fundamental difference. The younger generation, despite their shortcomings, are fundamentally better than their parents were at the same age, and certainly lack the conflicts engendered by Heathcliff's hostility toward Hindley and Edgar.

Study Questions

1. What makes Nelly suspicious about Cathy's behavior?
2. Who has been assisting Cathy in getting to the Heights?
3. How does Nelly react to Cathy's lie?
4. Who helps make Cathy's visits to Linton pleasant?
5. What different visions of heaven do Cathy and Linton have?
6. Why does Cathy call Hareton a "dunce"?
7. Of what does Nelly accuse Cathy?
8. Of whom does Linton remind Joseph, watching him pound at the door and scream?
9. What causes Cathy to forgive Linton?
10. What does Edgar consent to do for Linton?

Answers

1. Cathy makes unfounded excuses about being too tired to sit with Nelly as she convalesces, and thinking her behavior odd, Nelly goes to her room to discover it is empty.

2. Michael, the stable boy, has been assisting her, but Cathy admits she deceived him and asks that he not be reprimanded.

3. Nelly says she would rather be sick for another three months than to hear Cathy tell a lie.

4. Zillah is good-natured toward Cathy, providing refreshment and help when she visits.

5. Linton wants to lie in "an ecstasy of peace," while Cathy wants "all to sparkle, and dance in glorious jubilee."

6. Hareton has not yet learned his figures and has only just learned to spell his own name.

7. Hearing that Cathy laughed at Hareton, Nelly accuses her of very bad manners.

8. Joseph laughs and says, "Thear that's t' father!"

9. Linton apologizes, blaming his own unworthiness, and saying he loves her for her gentle goodness.

10. Edgar consents to write Linton a letter saying that while Cathy cannot return to the Heights, he is welcome to visit her at the Grange.

Suggested Essay Topics

1. In an earlier scene, Hareton hangs a litter of puppies while in Chapter 24, he reacts like a rebuked puppy. To what extent is a puppy an apt metaphor for Hareton?

2. How are the love triangles between Hareton-Cathy-Linton and Heathcliff-Catherine-Edgar similar? What is the fundamental difference?

Chapters 25–26

Summary

Conversing with Lockwood, Nelly reveals her awareness that he has fallen in love with Cathy himself. While Lockwood admits that might be true, he intends to resist the temptation, since he will eventually be returning to London and cannot afford a romantic complication. He asks Nelly to continue her narration.

Cathy has obeyed her father's restrictions. Edgar muses aloud over Linton to Nelly, asking her opinion of his suitability as a husband for Cathy. Believing he is too delicate to reach manhood, Nelly says if he does, at least Cathy would be able to control him. Edgar explains his concerns to Nelly. He knows he will soon die, and although he looks forward to an eternity beside Catherine, he worries about what will happen to Cathy. He can accept with equanimity the fact that a marriage between her and Linton will allow Heathcliff to inherit all his land. Edgar's only concern is if Linton can possibly make her happy. If his suspicions about Linton are correct, that he is "only a feeble tool to his father," he would rather "resign her to God, and lay her in the earth before me."

On Cathy's seventeenth birthday, he again writes to Linton, asking to see him. Linton responds that his father will not allow him to visit at the Grange, but hopes they can meet somewhere else. He begs Edgar to let him be with Cathy, since he is surrounded by people who dislike him, and requires her presence to be cheerful and well.

After some deliberation, Edgar consents to allow them to meet on the moors, with Nelly as chaperone. Edgar's hope is that the two will marry and come to live at the Grange, having no idea that Linton's death is as imminent as his own. Nelly adds that Linton's suggestion that they meet to walk or ride horseback is an indication of Linton's strength. She has no idea that in Heathcliff's eagerness to consummate his plan, he is only too willing to overtax Linton's precarious health.

On their date, Nelly and Cathy observe that Linton is so weak, he can barely stand. His lethargy is so severe that Cathy soon proposes to go home. This news makes Linton nervous, and glancing back toward the Heights, begs her to wait at least a half hour. Nelly senses that Linton is afraid of Heathcliff, and asks if he is treating the boy with "active" hatred. Unable to respond, Linton dozes off, leaving Cathy puzzled as to why he insisted on her remaining for half an hour. When she moves to leave, Linton awakens and tries to detain her, murmuring, "He's coming!" Cathy rides off before Heathcliff can arrive, promising to return the following Thursday.

Analysis

The contrasting motives of both fathers are evident in these chapters. Edgar, in his goodness, is resigned to relinquish all his property into the hands of his enemy, Heathcliff, if only he can guarantee his daughter's happiness. Centuries of family wealth and pride are meaningless to him, as long as his beloved child's future will be secure.

Heathcliff, on the other hand, views Linton merely as a pawn to advance his revenge against the Lintons and Earnshaws. He cares nothing for Linton's condition, desiring only the money he can gain through Linton's marriage to Cathy.

It is difficult at this point in the novel to recall any sympathy the reader may have had for Heathcliff in previous chapters. Consumed as he is with vengeance, he appears to be the embodiment of evil.

Study Questions

1. What surprises Nelly about the passage of time?

2. How does Nelly know Lockwood has fallen in love with Cathy?

3. Does Nelly believe that Linton will soon die?

4. What is unusual about Cathy's seventeenth birthday?

5. How does Cathy mistake her father's condition?

6. Of what does Linton wish to convince Edgar?

7. What shocks Cathy and Nelly when they meet Linton in the moor?

8. Why can we assume Linton insists on Cathy waiting half an hour?

9. What excuses for his poor condition does Linton ask Cathy to give her father?

10. Why can we assume Linton wants Cathy to misrepresent his condition to Edgar?

Answers

1. It has only been a year since the events in these two chapters occurred, and Nelly can hardly believe they have become material for the story she is telling a stranger.

2. Nelly believes that to see Cathy is to love her; Lockwood has also requested that her portrait be hung in his room.

3. Nelly thinks Linton's death is several years off.

4. Edgar puts off his customary visit to Catherine's grave.

5. Cathy believes her father's flushed cheeks and bright eyes are a sign of his convalescence.

6. Linton wants Edgar to see that he resembles Edgar more than Heathcliff.

7. Linton is so pale and feeble that he can barely stand.

8. It can be assumed by Linton's nervousness, and his glancing back toward the Heights, that Heathcliff is planning to join them.

9. Linton wants her to attribute his lethargy to the heat and unaccustomed exercise.

10. Linton fears that if Edgar knows how ill he is, he won't let Cathy marry him, angering Heathcliff.

Suggested Essay Topics

1. Discuss the way Edgar and Heathcliff treat their children.

2. Do you think it is symbolic that Edgar did not visit Catherine's grave on Cathy's seventeenth birthday?

Chapter 27

Summary

A week has gone by since Cathy and Linton's strange encounter. Edgar's condition continues to deteriorate, and Cathy is loath to leave his bedside in order to keep her date with Linton. Edgar insists that she go. He has no idea of Linton's detestable character, and Nelly hasn't the heart to tell him.

Cathy and Nelly return to the appointed meeting place to discover Linton in hysterical fear of Heathcliff. He begs Cathy to remain with him, intimating that Heathcliff will punish him for her refusal. Upon his arrival, Heathcliff confirms with Nelly that Edgar will die quickly, he blames Linton for not encouraging Cathy's affections. Tartly, Nelly points out that Linton needs to be under a doctor's care, not rambling around pretending to be lively.

Viciously, Heathcliff orders Linton to get up. Shaken Linton begs for Cathy's assistance, and Heathcliff tells her to help him walk home. Cathy demurs, saying she can't disobey her father by entering Heathcliff's house, so Heathcliff tells Nelly to bring Linton in. Nelly is reluctant to leave Cathy alone with Heathcliff, but when Heathcliff threatens to harm Linton, the women have no choice but to escort him into the house. Once they cross the threshold, Heathcliff locks them in.

Grabbing the key half out of Heathcliff's hand, Cathy infuriates Heathcliff. He orders her to stop, but when she persists, he strikes her several times. Grimly, Heathcliff tells Nelly he knows how to discipline unruly children, and promises Cathy more of the same if she ever displays her temper to him again. Handing Nelly a cup of tea, Heathcliff goes out to look for the horses she and Cathy left behind.

Furious, Cathy and Nelly demand that Linton tell them what is going on. Linton reveals Heathcliff's plan: afraid that Linton will predecease Edgar, Cathy will be forced to marry Linton in the morning, before she will be allowed to return to her dying father. Determined to get back to Edgar, Cathy says she will burn down the door if need be. Alarmed, Linton begs her to obey his father, but Cathy insists on obeying her own father, who she is certain must already be worried about her failure to return. Heathcliff reenters; the horses have run off. Seeing how abject Linton appears, he orders him to bed.

Alone with the two women, Heathcliff taunts Cathy for her obvious fear of him. Admitting that she is afraid, she nevertheless beseeches him to let her go home to relieve her father's concerns, promising to return in the morning to be married. Heathcliff assures her that the more anguish Edgar endures, the happier he will be. He further torments Cathy by promising her a life of tearful misery, for he has taught Linton to "play the little tyrant well."

As darkness falls, three servants from the Grange come searching for the women whose riderless horses have wandered home. Unaware of what is happening, Cathy and Nelly do not call for help, and Heathcliff hurries outside to send them away. Miserable at having missed the opportunity to be saved, Cathy and Nelly collapse in grief as Heathcliff locks them in a bedroom. In the morning, her jailor removes Cathy, but keeps Nelly imprisoned for four days, unable to obtain any information from Hareton when he brings her food.

Analysis

The main purpose of this chapter is to advance the plot, which is leading inexorably towards the fulfillment of Heathcliff's plans. The reader senses that Cathy is doomed. There is no one, except Hareton, who is capable of saving her, and he is clearly unwilling to cross Heathcliff.

The reader may also be numbed, at this point, to the degree of inhuman cruelty of which Heathcliff is capable. Prior to Catherine's death, his behavior still contained some redeeming features: he was capable of sincere and pure adoration, an emotion which normally enhances one's humanity. For Heathcliff, however, the frustration of unfulfilled love has debased his humanity. Are we then to regard Heathcliff solely as a demonic figure, a one-dimensional symbol of man's evil nature? The temptation is there, particularly after the preceding several chapters, to view him as exactly that. To do so, however, is to ignore what Brontë has in store. We must trust that the novel's conclusion will restore some of the compassion she enabled us to feel for him in earlier chapters.

Study Questions

1. Whom does Edgar believe Linton takes after?

2. Of what does Cathy accuse Linton when she comes to meet him?

3. What reason does Linton give for wanting her to stay?

4. Why is Heathcliff interested in learning how long Edgar is expected to live?

5. What directions have Heathcliff given Linton about how to behave with Cathy?

6. How does Nelly respond when Heathcliff asks her to take Linton inside?

7. How does Heathcliff induce Cathy and Nelly to enter the house?

8. What does Heathcliff say he would do to Linton and Cathy, if he lived in a less civilized country?

9. Why do the servants at the Grange search for Cathy and Nelly?

10. Who brings Nelly food while she is imprisoned?

Answers

1. Edgar incorrectly believes that Linton not only resembles him physically, but in terms of his good character, as well.

2. Cathy accuses Linton of wasting her time, which could be better spent with her father, especially since he doesn't seem particularly pleased to see her.

3. Linton says that Heathcliff has threatened him if he cannot succeed in keeping Cathy there this time, and he is in terror of his temper.

4. Heathcliff is unsure of Linton's life expectancy, and wants to make certain Edgar dies before him.

5. Heathcliff has told Linton not to "snivel," and to be lively instead.

6. Nelly tells Heathcliff his son is not her business, and she dare not leave Cathy alone with him.

7. He prevails on Cathy to lead Linton inside to a chair, and while Nelly waits for her on the threshold, Heathcliff pushes her inside, shuts and locks the door.

8. He would treat himself to "a slow vivisection of those two, as an evening's entertainment."

9. Their horses have returned riderless, and they could not be found anywhere on the Grange estate.

10. Hareton brings her food, but refuses to give her any information.

Suggested Essay Topics

1. At this point in the novel, argue whether or not you think Heathcliff is a redeemable character.

2. If Heathcliff truly loved Catherine, why do you think he treats Cathy, her own daughter, in such a horrible way? After seeing the way he treats Linton and Hareton, do you think he would treat Cathy differently if he, not Edgar, was her father?

Chapters 28–29

New Character:

Mr. Green: *a lawyer*

Summary

Rumor in the village has it that Nelly and Cathy had been rescued by Heathcliff from drowning in a marsh, and that they have been recuperating at Wuthering Heights. This information is relayed to Nelly by Zillah when she unlocks the door for her. Zillah also brings Nelly a message from Heathcliff: she is to go at once to the Grange and Cathy will follow her in time for Edgar's funeral. Aghast to think that Edgar has died alone, Nelly is told that he has perhaps another day to live. She hurries out, looking around to see if Cathy is there.

Linton is the only one around. Lying on a couch, he indolently sucks on a stick of candy as he tells Nelly that Cathy has been sobbing since their forced marriage. Seeing that he has no compassion for Cathy, Nelly berates him for having forgotten all her kindness to him. Linton is unmoved; he now owns everything that is Cathy's, he childishly boasts. He and Heathcliff have even taken her locket with a picture of her parents away from her, just to reinforce the point that she no longer owns anything. Linton alarms Nelly even further when he tells her that Heathcliff has hit her hard enough to draw blood.

Wasting no time, Nelly rushes back to the Grange both to reassure Edgar that Cathy will soon come, and to hire a lawyer, Mr. Green, to alter Edgar's will in order to prevent Heathcliff from having legal claim to Cathy's inheritance. Then she sends a posse of four strong men to the Heights to have them force Heathcliff into returning Cathy.

Nelly is thwarted in both efforts. The four men return without Cathy, having stupidly believed Heathcliff's story that she is too ill to travel. Even worse, Mr. Green has been paid off by Heathcliff to delay his arrival at the Grange until his services can no longer be of use. Luckily, Cathy has finally convinced Linton to help her escape. She climbs out the window of her mother's former room, and rushes to the Grange in time to bid her dying father farewell.

Edgar, however, has died before he could change his will. Everything that Edgar has left to Cathy now legally belongs to Linton, who will leave it to Heathcliff. Mr. Green arrives, and under Heathcliff's orders, dismisses all the servants except Nelly. He even attempts to prevent Edgar's coffin from being buried next to Catherine's, but that provision has been legally assured.

Heathcliff emerges to take Cathy back to the Heights, warning her not to try to run away again. Nelly implores him to let Cathy remain and have Linton join her. Heathcliff prefers, however, to watch them suffer and increase his wealth by renting out the Grange. Proudly, Cathy tells Heathcliff that she intends to love Linton; he is all she has now. Before she leaves, she retaliates somewhat, reminding him that for all his vengeful satisfaction, he is miserable because he has nobody to love him.

Alone with Nelly, Heathcliff demands Catherine's portrait be sent to the Heights. Slyly, he tells her that while Edgar's grave was being dug, he pried the lid of Catherine's coffin so that he could see her face again. He also altered her coffin so that when he dies he can be laid next to Catherine as well. Appalled that he would

disturb the dead, Nelly is sharp with him, but he promises her this will insure his spirit, unlike Catherine's, of remaining peacefully in the grave once he is dead. He galls Nelly by telling her how he dug up Catherine's dead body the night after her funeral so he could embrace her again.

Continuing his delusions about Catherine, Heathcliff does not stop until Cathy comes in to tell him she is ready to leave once her pony is saddled. Pitiless, Heathcliff tells her the pony will not be needed; she will not be going anywhere once she has returned to the Heights. In addition, he forbids Nelly from seeing Cathy, and, taking her arm, leads her away.

Analysis

Two issues are worth noting in these chapters: one is Brontë's legal acumen. The information Nelly gives us about Edgar's hopes to circumnavigate Heathcliff's claims on his property are so detailed that the reader must be impressed with Brontë's knowledge of English inheritance laws. According to *The Scribner's Companion to the Brontës*, an English lawyer who examined the complicated legal process by which Heathcliff gained his property found that Brontë's knowledge was astonishingly accurate, not for the 1840's when the novel was written, but for the late eighteenth century, when the novel actually took place. This strongly suggests extensive research on Brontë's part (Evans 309).

Another issue worth noting is Heathcliff's revelation that he has twice disturbed Catherine's grave. Earlier in the novel Heathcliff's sanity has been questioned, both by Isabella who asked if he was human or simply mad, and by Nelly who at times described him as ghoulish. There is no doubt that his obsession with Catherine's dead body touches on ghoulish insanity. However, it must be remembered that in addition to his lust for vengeance, Heathcliff also longs to have his soul at peace. He has exacted his vengeance by ruining Hindley and debasing both his and Edgar's descendants. Now he awaits peace, which he can only have with Catherine.

Study Questions

1. What does Zillah believe has happened to Nelly?

2. Why does Nelly tell Linton she is shedding tears?

3. How does Linton stand to see Heathcliff strike Cathy?

4. How does Edgar plan to alter his will?

5. After the four men return without Cathy, what does Nelly resolve to do?

6. Why was the lawyer late in responding to Nelly's summons?

7. Why does Heathcliff believe Cathy will learn to hate Linton?

8. What happened the night of Catherine's funeral?

9. What has been killing Heathcliff slowly, over the years?

10. Why can't Cathy bring her pony to the Heights?

Answers

1. Zillah has heard in the village that Nelly was sinking into Blackhorse Marsh, until Heathcliff saved her and brought her to the Heights.

2. Nelly is grieved that Linton is ignoring Cathy's misery, after all of her kindness and attention to him.

3. He winks; he does so whenever Heathcliff exhibits physical cruelty.

4. Instead of leaving his money to Cathy, Edgar will put it in trust for her to use for herself or any future children.

5. Nelly resolves to return at dawn with an army of men, if need be.

6. The lawyer is now in Heathcliff's employ, and Heathcliff had ordered him to delay his arrival until Edgar's death.

7. Heathcliff says he won't have to try to make her hate Linton; his own "sweet spirit" will make him hateful to her.

8. Heathcliff dug up her grave, determined to warm her in his arms. He senses the breath of a living being, even though he is alone, and realizes that Catherine's spirit is with him.

9. He dreams constantly that Catherine is with him, but when he opens his eyes, she is gone. Frustrated in his hope of seeing her has slowly brought him close to death.

10. Heathcliff tells Cathy that the only journeys she will be taking from now on will be on foot.

Suggested Essay Topics

1. Although it seems Heathcliff has been awarded his revenge, Cathy continues to defy him. Give examples of Cathy's defiance of Heathcliff.

2. Explain Heathcliff's obsession with Catherine's dead body. Argue whether he is insane or is determined to be at peace by opening Catherine's grave.

Chapters 30–31

Summary

Attempting to see Cathy, Nelly is rebuffed by Joseph at the door. However, Zillah often meets Nelly in town, and through her, Nelly is kept informed of the events at the Heights.

Cathy appears and reports Zillah, very haughty and unfriendly, choosing to remain in Linton's company only. Occasionally catching a glimpse of the girl in tears, Zillah hardens herself against becoming involved. She does not wish to antagonize Heathcliff by befriending Cathy against his orders. Nevertheless, one night Cathy rushes into Zillah's room demanding that Heathcliff be sent for; Linton is dying, for certain. Afraid to disturb Heathcliff, Zillah ignores her, but the ringing of Linton's bedside bell eventually sends her into Heathcliff's room.

Heathcliff finds Cathy sitting numbly beside Linton's corpse, and asks her how she feels. "He's safe, and I'm free," she replies, but adds that she feels like death. She remains in seclusion for fifteen days, visited only by Zillah, whose overtures at kindness are proudly repelled. Heathcliff visits her once to show her Linton's will. Coerced by his father, Linton has, unsurprisingly, signed over all his and Cathy's assets to Heathcliff. Although Linton could not

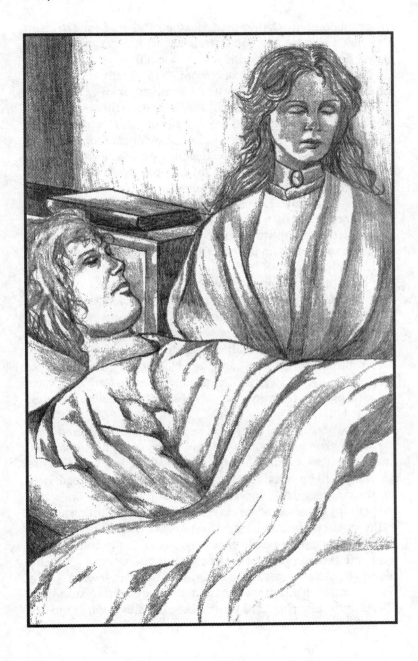

legally meddle with Cathy's land, Heathcliff has managed to claim it as well, using his position as Isabella's widower. Cathy is completely destitute and dependent on Heathcliff.

Nearly frozen in her solitary room, Cathy finally ventures into the warm kitchen one Sunday when Heathcliff is away. Zillah and Hareton attempt to be friendly, but Cathy assures them she is there for the warmth, not the company; neither of them helped her take care of Linton nor offered her any comfort before, so she views their overtures as hypocrisy. Hareton eagerly informs her that he had tried to help her, but Heathcliff always denied him the opportunity. Cathy refuses to hear his excuses.

Zillah's narrative ends here. Nelly resolves to quit her position at the Grange, obtain a small cottage, and take Cathy to live with her, but Heathcliff thwarts her hope.

Lockwood picks up the narrative, informing the reader of the rapid improvement of his health. He visits the Heights to tell Heathcliff of his decision to make an early departure for London. Told that Heathcliff will be returning shortly, Lockwood waits in the kitchen under Hareton's supervision, and observes that Cathy appears so lethargic, he fails to see how her disposition deserves Nelly's praise. Nevertheless, he kindly drops a letter from Nelly in her lap, but she brushes it away without looking at it. Hareton picks it up, insisting that Heathcliff must read it before Cathy can have it. Catching sight of Cathy's teary eyes, Hareton relents and hands over the letter.

Lockwood informs Cathy that he feels as if he knows her; Nelly has spoken so much about her. Cathy responds to him at last, informing him that Heathcliff has destroyed all her books. She blames Hareton, thinking he is jealous of her because he cannot read. With gentlemanly etiquette, Lockwood defends Hareton's feelings, saying perhaps he merely wishes to emulate Cathy by learning to read. Cathy mocks Hareton's attempts to learn, but Lockwood points out that every beginner needs encouragement. Cathy continues to denigrate Hareton's efforts until he storms out, returning with his hidden books and tossing them into Cathy's lap. Jeering, Cathy reads aloud from one of the books, mimicking Hareton's stumbling efforts. Infuriated, he grabs the books and tosses them in the fire.

Heathcliff returns as Hareton runs out. Gazing after him, Heathcliff is moved by the young man's strong physical resemblance to his beloved Catherine. Noticing Lockwood, Heathcliff congratulates him on his improved health. Learning of Lockwood's plan to leave the Grange prematurely, Heathcliff warns him there will be no refund on the rent. Exasperated, Lockwood replies that his is not seeking one. Invited to dinner, Lockwood endures a silent meal with Heathcliff and Hareton; Cathy is banished to the kitchen to eat.

Failing to catch a final glimpse of Cathy before he departs, Lockwood muses about his lost opportunity to romance the girl, and rescue her from her dreary life, as Nelly had hoped.

Analysis

Sadly, Cathy's declaration to Heathcliff that Linton's death has made her free is ironic, for she is now completely dependent on her worst enemy for her food and shelter. The reader can empathize with her intense frustration; only seventeen years old, she is penniless and alone, a prisoner of a man who harbors malevolent hatred for her. It is no wonder that Cathy lashes at out at Hareton, the only person who she senses will not harm her. Perhaps the reader will find evidence in her treatment of Hareton of her mother Catherine's ability to be mocking and inflict pain. Cathy, it must be remembered, has generally emulated Edgar's tendency to be kind, while Catherine's motivations were always self-serving.

Brontë has taken care to show the reader that the second generation does not replicate its parents. Hareton, although uncouth, has none of Hindley's vicious and degenerate behavior. In fact, his kindness toward Linton and Cathy has been mentioned throughout the book. Furthermore, everybody seems to like Hareton, even Heathcliff, who is drawn to the boy whose life he saved in infancy and subsequently tried to destroy. If Cathy's hostility toward Hareton can be resolved, there is a hope for the redemption of the second generation of Earnshaws and Lintons.

Study Questions

1. Why is Zillah so unfriendly towards Cathy?

2. Who aides Cathy in nursing Linton?

3. How does Hareton react to Linton's death?

4. Why does Zillah remain behind when Heathcliff is gone and Joseph is at church?

5. What does Hareton do while Cathy sits reading by the fire?

6. Why is Cathy forced to sit in the kitchen with Hareton and Zillah?

7. What decision does Lockwood make concerning the Grange?

8. Why can Cathy not answer Nelly's letter?

9. How does Lockwood try to spare Hareton's feelings?

10. How does Heathcliff react to the news of Lockwood's departure?

Answers

1. Heathcliff has ordered her to let Cathy look after herself; furthermore, Zillah finds Cathy haughty.

2. She is told that nursing Linton is her job, so no one helps Cathy, even when she appears confused and overwhelmed.

3. Hareton is more concerned with staring at Cathy than thinking about Linton.

4. Zillah realizes that Hareton is attracted to Cathy, and feels it proper that the two young people not be left alone.

5. Hareton becomes entranced by the curl of hair brushing Cathy's cheek, and attempts to stroke it.

6. Her bedroom is unheated. Since it is the dead of winter, Cathy finds the cold unbearable and sits in the kitchen to get warm.

7. Lockwood decides he has had enough of Yorkshire winters, and will return to London for the next six months.

8. Cathy has no paper on which to write, not even a book she could tear a page from.

9. Lockwood praises Hareton's efforts at learning to read, and soothingly reminds him that every beginner stumbles at first.

10. Heathcliff assumes Lockwood is tired of living in a desolate area, but warns him that he will not refund him any rent.

Suggested Essay Topics

1. Write an analysis of Cathy. Argue whether or not she is a sympathetic character. Is she willful and spoiled?

2. Brontë clearly had impressive knowledge of early nineteenth century English inheritance laws. Research American inheritance laws in the late twentieth century, comparing the difference in the role of women.

Chapters 32–33

Summary

It is September 1802. Visiting a friend in northern England, Lockwood realizes he is only fourteen miles away from Thrushcross Grange. Acting on impulse, he decides to spend the night there, since he is still paying rent to Heathcliff for the house. On arriving, he meets an unfamiliar servant who tells him Nelly has moved into Wuthering Heights. Curious, Lockwood walks over to see how everyone is doing.

There is something different about the formerly foreboding place. The gate is no longer locked against visitors, and flowers bloom profusely in the garden. Most strangely, he spies Cathy and Hareton engaged in a reading lesson interrupted by kisses and other signs of affection.

Unseen, Lockwood slides past them into the kitchen where Nelly sits singing as she sews. She is delighted to see Lockwood again, but is surprised to discover that he is unaware of Heathcliff's death three months ago. As Lockwood sips some ale, she narrates the story of his "queer" death.

Two weeks after Lockwood's departure, Nelly is summoned to the Heights. Heathcliff explains that he no longer wishes to see Cathy, so he wants Nelly to move in and make a small apartment

for herself and the girl. The arrangement soon proves unsatisfactory. Cathy resents being confined to a small space all day, and is reduced to fighting with Joseph in the kitchen. Hareton also frequents the kitchen, where he continues to be the victim of Cathy's scorn.

One day, Cathy relents, and offers to let Hareton try to read one of her books. When he rebuffs her offer, she leaves the book beside him. Still unable to make amends, Cathy finally approaches Hareton, and awkwardly proposes to become friends, despite her awareness that he has always hated her. Furious at being faulted, Hareton claims that he has risked Heathcliff's wrath often in taking her part, only to have endured her constant ridicule. Eventually, her persistence overcomes his damaged pride, and the cousins sit together looking at a book. An affectionate relationship rapidly develops.

Nelly interrupts herself to admit to Lockwood that she is glad he did not try to win Cathy's love, since a wedding between Cathy and Hareton now seems inevitable. It will be, reports Nelly, "the crown of all her wishes."

Returning to the events of three months earlier, Nelly relates how Cathy has persuaded Hareton to dig up some old currant trees (favorites of Joseph), and replace them with flowers transplanted from the Grange. Later at a meal, Nelly notes that Cathy has decided not to hide their relationship from Heathcliff any longer, and flirts with Hareton at the table. Heathcliff shoots a surly glance at the pair, but says nothing until Joseph bursts in, screaming about the loss of "his" trees. Learning that is was Cathy's idea, Heathcliff turns on her for having touched his property. Emboldened, Cathy points out that Heathcliff has not only stolen everything from her, but from Hareton as well. When Cathy threatens to use her influence to turn Hareton against him, Heathcliff orders Hareton to get rid of her. Clearly torn between his loyalty to Heathcliff and his love for Cathy, Hareton begs her to stop. She refuses, and Heathcliff grabs her by the hair. Intervening, Hareton pleads with him not to hurt her. Shaken, Heathcliff lets her go, and calmly tells her to avoid provoking him. Warning Hareton not to be influenced by Cathy unless he wants to be turned out, Heathcliff allows the scene to end without violence.

Alone later in the house, Hareton tells Cathy he will not endure any criticisms of Heathcliff, to whom Hareton is unquestionably devoted. Astounded at first by his attachment to the man who ruined him, Cathy realizes that Hareton regards Heathcliff as a father figure, and to try to convince him of Heathcliff's injustice would be more cruel than helpful.

Reconciled, the two continue with their reading lessons. Observing them, Nelly reflects on her hand in both their upbringing; as the only mother either has ever known, she regards them both as her children. She is proud of them: Hareton's innate goodness has helped him overcome his childhood of neglect and violence, while Cathy has outgrown her juvenile petulance, and is now a worthy young woman.

While Nelly is thinking this over, Heathcliff returns. As the two look up Heathcliff is overwhelmed by their mutual resemblance to Catherine. Composing himself, he bids them leave the room, but asks Nelly to remain. In a lengthy soliloquy, Heathcliff dwells on the ironic conclusion to his plan for revenge. After nearly a lifetime devoted to the destruction of the Earnshaws and Lintons, he finds himself disinclined to impinge on Hareton's and Cathy's happiness. This is not due to any generosity on his part; it is just that hurting them has ceased to give him satisfaction. He senses a significant change in himself in that all of his vengeful passion has turned into complete apathy.

While Cathy is truly insignificant to Heathcliff, Hareton moves him deeply. The young man reminds him of himself as a youth, yet if it could be managed, Heathcliff would prefer to avoid him, since Hareton's strong resemblance to Catherine is a constant reminder of his loss.

Listening to him, Nelly seizes on his use of the word "change." Viewing him as sound of mind as she, excepting his obsession with Catherine, she is alarmed to think that the change he refers to is death. He tells her he is not ill. Life, however, has become too difficult to endure. The attainment of his revenge has lost its meaning, and he is left exhausted by the struggle, wishing only that it were over.

Analysis

These chapters contain a certain poignance. The reader cannot help but be moved by Hareton's unwavering devotion to Heathcliff. It must be recalled that Hareton is basically unaware of how he has been cheated; furthermore, Heathcliff represents the only father Hareton has ever really known. Hindley, we recall, frequently terrorized the child while drunk, and died before Hareton could have tried to understand the causes of his father's misery. Heathcliff, on the other hand, has always demonstrated a gruff affection for the boy, and in fact, tells us in Chapter 33 that he views Hareton as "a personification of my youth."

It is touching, as well, to observe Cathy's increasing maturity. She has the capability to use Hareton's love for her as a tool against Heathcliff, but she wisely chooses not to. She recognizes that Hareton needs to believe in Heathcliff, and is content to allow Hareton's attachment to Heathcliff remain.

Most important, it is in these chapters that Heathcliff reclaims our sympathy. Lives have been gravely altered by his machinations; certain Hindley's ruination was at Heathcliff's hand. Had Brontë permitted Heathcliff to achieve the complete ruination of the two families, we might well be tempted to write him off as a purely evil monster. However, Brontë makes it clear that redemption is at hand for Hareton and Cathy—the second generation. Flowers, transplanted from Thrushcross Grange, flourish in the soil of Wuthering Heights, symbolizing the transference of goodness to a house of abject misery. Unbarred gates replace the sealed jail-like atmosphere. Hareton has been saved from a life of ignorance and poverty, tutored by Cathy into literacy, and returned by Heathcliff's death to his position. The love and devotion Cathy knew from her father has been restored by her impending marriage. Ultimately, Heathcliff himself no longer sees the meaning in his revenge. It is because of this that he decides to focus on the afterlife, where he and Catherine can be reunited.

Study Questions

1. How long has Lockwood been away from Yorkshire?
2. What is different about Hareton's appearance?

3. About what do Nelly and Joseph argue?

4. Why did Heathcliff remove Nelly from the Grange?

5. How does Cathy tempt Hareton into accepting her book?

6. In what manner does Cathy finally win Hareton over?

7. Why does Nelly advise Cathy to be discrete about Hareton?

8. Why is Joseph angry at Hareton?

9. What does Hareton tell Cathy regarding Heathcliff?

10. What change in himself does Heathcliff sense?

Answers

1. Lockwood is returning after three months.

2. Hareton is respectably dressed and apparently very happy.

3. Joseph finds Nelly's singing sinful; he is also bothered by Hareton's transformation.

4. Heathcliff wants her to live in the Heights in order to keep Cathy away from his sight.

5. Cathy reads out loud in Hareton's presence, stopping at an interesting part, and leaving the open book lying about.

6. Cathy gives Hareton a kiss, despite Nelly's disapproving look, and then presents him with a gift-wrapped book.

7. Nelly knows the budding romance will annoy him greatly.

8. Joseph is angry that Hareton has obeyed Cathy's wishes to dig up his currant trees and plant flowers instead.

9. Hareton would rather Cathy speak against him than Heathcliff.

10. Heathcliff senses his life has lost its purpose. Catherine was the only person who meant anything to him, and his revenge has not been as satisfying as he had imagined.

Suggested Essay Topics

1. Discuss Heathcliff's and Hareton's relationship.

2. What does the replacement of the currant trees for flowers symbolize?

Chapter 34

Summary

Following his discussion with Nelly, Heathcliff fails to show up for his meals, shunning all company. Nelly learns that he has been walking outdoors all night.

One morning, Cathy is startled by Heathcliff's return, reporting to Hareton and Nelly that Heathcliff actually spoke to her without his customary threatening manner. Indeed, she could swear he seemed excited and cheerful! Concerned and confused, Nelly decides to investigate. She, too, notices "a strange, joyful glitter in his eyes." Refusing breakfast, Heathcliff asks to be left alone.

At noon, he accepts a full plate of food, declaring himself ready to eat at last. However after a few mouthfuls, he pushes the food away, and paces outside in the garden, as a perplexed Hareton tries to find out what the problem is. Hareton, too, finds Heathcliff in a rare, happy mood, although Heathcliff asks Hareton to leave him in solitude.

When he returns an hour or two later, Nelly remarks on the unnatural, chilling appearance of Heathcliff's face; he is pale, and shivering from nervous agitation. Nelly begs him to let her know why he is acting so strangely—has he had good news? Heathcliff reports that he is "within sight of heaven," and repeats his desire to be left alone.

No one disturbs him in his room, until Nelly attempts to bring him food at eight that night. Nelly is truly panicked at how Heathcliff looks; he appears to be a goblin, not a man. Feeling foolish, but terrified, she runs out. "Is he a ghoul or a vampire?" she ponders. Reminding herself that she has known Heathcliff since he was a small child, Nelly tries to rationalize her unease. She spends a fitful night trying to make sense of Heathcliff's suspicious origins, and eventually dreams of his death and funeral. She is disturbed that she, his confidant for nearly forty years, does not know his surname or the date of his birth, and therefore his tombstone can be inscribed only with his single name and the date of his death.

By morning, Nelly feels calmer, until Heathcliff appears for breakfast and continues in his strange behavior. Ignoring the coffee she puts before him, he smiles at some unseen vision, his face so ghastly that Nelly cries out. Heathcliff tells her to be quiet, and asks if they are alone, despite the fact that the kitchen is obviously empty except for them. Brushing away the food, Heathcliff leans across the table, continuing to stare at something that Nelly cannot see. Finally, he leaves and does not return until after midnight.

Awake when he returns, Nelly hears him call, "Catherine," speaking as if Catherine were indeed beside him. Too frightened to confront him, she remains in her bed until dawn, when he summons her. He wants her to send for Mr. Green, the lawyer, so that he can write a will, although he does not yet know how he will dispose of his property. Nelly advises him to wait until he has eaten and rested; the past three days have taken their toll on his nerves. Heathcliff says he cannot rest until he "reaches what is waiting" for him, and then changes his mind about writing a will.

Unable to understand Heathcliff's mystical speech, Nelly advises him to send for a minister, and seek salvation from the Bible, fearing that he will be unfit for heaven unless he does. Rejecting the idea of a minister, Heathcliff thanks her nevertheless for reminding him of how he wishes to be buried. He wants only her and Hareton to accompany his coffin to the churchyard, warning her to obey his earlier instructions about being buried next to Catherine, unless she wants to be haunted by his angry spirit.

That night, everyone hears Heathcliff groaning and murmuring in his room. Hareton and Nelly decide to send for the doctor, but when he knocks at the door, Heathcliff curses and sends him away.

The following evening, during a pouring rain, Nelly observes the window to Heathcliff's room swinging open. Running upstairs to look, Nelly sees Heathcliff's dead body drenched with rain, on the bed. Kneeling at his side, Nelly tries to close the dead man's eyes, but rigor mortis has set in. His entire face is frozen in a contemptible sneer. Joseph comes in, but refuses to touch Heathcliff, saying the devil has finally carried him off. Falling to his knees,

Joseph prays, thanking heaven for returning Hareton to his lawful position in his ancient family.

Despite the gossip it incurs, Heathcliff is buried as he had requested, on one side of Catherine. Edgar's grave remains on her other side. Hareton weeps as he digs the grave.

Her long narrative finally drawing to a close, Nelly tells Lockwood that many, Joseph included, believe Heathcliff haunts the moors. A little shepherd boy has told Nelly of seeing Heathcliff and a woman standing on the road. While she claims not to believe this, she admits to being too frightened to venture outdoors at night, and eagerly awaits Hareton and Cathy's marriage on New Year's, so she can move back to the Grange.

Lockwood walks back to spend his final night at the Grange before returning to London. Looking up at the sky, he enjoys the scent of flowers and the breeze, wondering about the restless souls beneath him.

Analysis

While everyone else in the family is taken aback at Heathcliff's "queer" state, the reader has a fair idea that Catherine's spirit has at last made contact with Heathcliff. It is undoubtedly at her he stares while in the kitchen with Nelly, and it is surely she to whom he speaks as he mounts the stairs at night. As Catherine was the only joy Heathcliff has ever known, only she could have produced in him the uncharacteristic happiness and agitation noticed by the others.

The culmination of Heathcliff's life, therefore, is not in revenge against Hindley and the Lintons. We can assume he has considered writing a will in order to restore at least Hareton's if not Cathy's inheritances. He rejects the idea of calling the lawyer, finally, because he can think of nothing but in finding peace and fulfillment with Catherine. Since this can only happen once he is dead, he awaits death with some impatience, content to know he will soon be spending eternity at Catherine's side.

Study Questions

1. What time of year does Heathcliff's death take place?

2. What perplexes Cathy about Heathcliff's behavior?

3. For how many days does Heathcliff bewilder everyone?

4. How does Heathcliff respond to Nelly's asking him why he is behaving so oddly?

5. Why does Nelly decide she is being foolish to wonder if Heathcliff is a ghoul or a vampire?

6. About what do Joseph and Heathcliff converse?

7. To what does Nelly attribute Heathcliff's unseen vision?

8. What does Heathcliff say he wishes he could do with his property?

9. What has Heathcliff died from?

10. How does Lockwood bid Nelly goodbye?

Answers

1. Heathcliff dies in April, when the weather was "warm and sweet."

2. Although Heathcliff still tells Nelly to get out of his sight, he looks so excited and happy she hardly recognizes him.

3. Heathcliff has been behaving "queerly" for three days.

4. Heathcliff tells Nelly that the previous night he was on the "threshold of hell," but today, he is in "sight of my heaven."

5. Nelly has tended Heathcliff since infancy, and has known him well through most of his life.

6. Heathcliff discusses some farming business with Joseph, but speaks rapidly and continually turns his head from side to side.

7. Heathcliff has not eaten for days, and Nelly attributes his hallucinations to this.

8. Heathcliff wishes he could "annihilate it from the face of the earth."

9. Mr. Kenneth does not know what illness caused his death; Nelly believes his not having eaten was a symptom of the illness, not a cause of his death.

10. Lockwood presses some money into Nelly's hand, disregarding her protests, and walks back to Thrushcross Grange.

Suggested Essay Topics

1. Describe Heathcliff's death. Do you feel Heathcliff found peace?

2. Describe the characters' reactions to Heathcliff's death.

Sample Analytical Paper Topics

Topic #1

Wuthering Heights can be viewed as the struggle between civilized, conventional human behavior and its wild, anarchistic side. Put simply, the novel contrasts the good and evil in human nature.

Outline

I. Thesis Statement: *In* Wuthering Heights, *Brontë depicts the clash between good and evil in human nature.*

II. Thrushcross Grange and Wuthering Heights as representatives of good and evil

   A. The Grange—gracious and comfortable; its residents, Edgar and Isabella are conventional, kind, and well-mannered.

   B. The Heights—dark and foreboding; its residents Heathcliff, Hindley, and Catherine are selfish and wild.

III. Characters as contrasts in human nature

   A. Catherine and Edgar—she makes him miserable with her wild scenes and passionate attachment to Heathcliff, while she cannot thrive in his world of gentleness and order.

   B. Isabella and Heathcliff—Her romantic innocence is destroyed by his calculated use of her in order to gain his revenge.

IV. Conclusion

    A. Hareton—redeemed from the Earnshaw taint of savage brutishness by Cathy's love, is restored to his position by Heathcliff's death.

    B. Cathy—retaining her father's noble qualities, she submerges her mother's impetuous nature as she matures.

    C. The irreconcilable aspects of good and evil are resolved by the successful futures of the second generation family members.

Topic #2

Brontë is unusual as an author in her refusal to make value judgements about her characters. The reader is not entirely certain if Heathcliff is meant to be viewed as demonic or sympathetic. Decide which view the text best supports.

Outline

I. Thesis Statement: *Heathcliff is primarily a one-dimensional character, entirely evil, incapable of goodness.*

II. Heathcliff's evil

    A. Obsession with revenge

    B. Cold-blooded ruination of Hindley

    C. Destruction of Edgar's contentment

    D. Brutality towards Isabella and Linton

    E. Cheating Hareton and Cathy of their inheritances

III. Conclusion

    A. Heathcliff dies because his capacity to do further evil wanes.

    B. His spirit still haunts the moors, implying that he has never found peace.

Topic #3

From an early age, Heathcliff has experienced injustices. First, he was an orphan, living on the streets of Liverpool, when Mr. Earnshaw found him. The rest of the Earnshaw family is appalled of the idea of Heathcliff joining their family. Hindley is cruel to Heathcliff as a child, and Edgar refuses to allow Heathcliff and Catherine to be friends. Heathcliff's revenge later in life on the Earnshaw family may be justified.

Outline

I.   Thesis Statement: *Heathcliff, while embodying the evil side of human nature, was driven to revenge by the ill treatment he received.*

II.   Injustices done to Heathcliff

    A.   Hindley's childhood cruelty

    B.   Edgar's social disparagement

    C.   Hindley's humiliating treatment as an adult

    D.   Edgar's refusal to allow his friendship with Catherine

III. Conclusion

    A.   Heathcliff's evil nature can, to some extent, be justified.

    B.   His humanity is redeemed by his capacity to love Catherine.

    C.   Heathcliff's evil is revoked by his disinclination to interfere with Hareton's and Cathy's happiness.

    D.   He attains peace in the fulfillment of an afterlife spent with Catherine.

Topic #4

In Wuthering Heights, Brontë employs stylisitc devices such as symbolism and recurring motifs.

Outline

I.   Thesis Statement: *Brontë employs use of symbolism and motifs to add dimension of depth to* Wuthering Heights.

II. Symbolism

    A. Thrushcross Grange symbolizes civilization and gentility, with its well-tended grounds, gentle inhabitants, and gracious atmosphere.

    B. *Wuthering Heights* symbolizes decay and savagery, whipped by bitter northern winds, with its brutish residents and foreboding atmosphere.

III. Motifs

    A. Dogs

        1. Heathcliff's dog attacks Lockwood.

        2. Mr. Linton's dog attacks Catherine.

        3. Heathcliff hangs Isabella's dog.

        4. Little Hareton emulates Heathcliff by hanging a litter of puppies.

        5. Hareton is treated like a puppy, either patted or whipped.

    B. Windows

        1. Catherine's ghost tries to enter through a window.

        2. Catherine awaits Heathcliff while sitting by a window.

        3. Heathcliff holds vigil under Catherine's window.

        4. Window blows open at Heathcliff's death, suggesting the freeing of his tortured spirit.

IV. Conclusion: Stylistic devices such as symbolism and recurring motifs add a depth of understanding to the novel.

SECTION FOUR

Bibliography

Allen, Walter. *The English Novel.* New York: E.P. Dutton, 1955.

Benvenuto, Richard. *Emily Brontë.* Boston: Twayne Publishers, 1982.

"Emily Brontë." Nineteenth Century Literary Criticism. Ed. Cherie Abbey & Janet Mullane. vol 16. Detroit: Gale Research, 1987.

Evans, Barbara & Gareth Lloyd Evans. *The Scribner Companion to the Brontës.* New York: Chass. Scribner's Sons, 1982.

Karl, Frederick R. *An Age of Fiction; The Nineteenth Century British Novel.* New York: Farrar, Straus & Giroux, 1964.

Pool, Daniel. *What Jane Austen Ate and Charles Dickens Knew.* New York: Simon & Schuster, 1993.

Traversi, Derek. "The Brontë Sisters and *Wuthering Heights.*" *Twentieth Century Interpretations of Wuthering Heights.* Englewood Cliffs, NJ: Prentice Hall, 1968.

REA's Test Preps
The Best in Test Preparation

- REA "Test Preps" are far **more** comprehensive than any other test preparation series
- Each book contains up to **eight** full-length practice exams based on the most recent exams
- **Every** type of question likely to be given on the exams is included
- Answers are accompanied by **full** and **detailed** explanations

REA has published over 60 Test Preparation volumes in several series. They include:

Advanced Placement Exams (APs)
Biology
Calculus AB & Calculus BC
Chemistry
Computer Science
English Language & Composition
English Literature & Composition
European History
Government & Politics
Physics
Psychology
Spanish Language
United States History

**College Level Examination
 Program (CLEP)**
American History I
Analysis & Interpretation of
 Literature
College Algebra
Freshman College Composition
General Examinations
Human Growth and Development
Introductory Sociology
Principles of Marketing

SAT II: Subject Tests
American History
Biology
Chemistry
French
German
Literature

SAT II: Subject Tests (continued)
Mathematics Level IC, IIC
Physics
Spanish
Writing

Graduate Record Exams (GREs)
Biology
Chemistry
Computer Science
Economics
Engineering
General
History
Literature in English
Mathematics
Physics
Political Science
Psychology
Sociology

ACT - American College Testing
 Assessment

ASVAB - Armed Service Vocational
 Aptitude Battery

CBEST - California Basic Educational
 Skills Test

CDL - Commercial Driver's License Exam

CLAST - College Level Academic Skills
 Test

ELM - Entry Level Mathematics

ExCET - Exam for Certification of
 Educators in Texas

FE (EIT) - Fundamentals of
 Engineering Exam

FE Review - Fundamentals of
 Engineering Review

GED - High School Equivalency
 Diploma Exam (US & Canadian
 editions)

GMAT - Graduate Management
 Admission Test

LSAT - Law School Admission Test

MAT - Miller Analogies Test

MCAT - Medical College Admission
 Test

MSAT - Multiple Subjects
 Assessment for Teachers

NTE - National Teachers Exam

PPST - Pre-Professional Skills Tests

PSAT - Preliminary Scholastic
 Assessment Test

SAT I - Reasoning Test

SAT I - Quick Study & Review

TASP - Texas Academic Skills
 Program

TOEFL - Test of English as a
 Foreign Language

Available at your local bookstore or order directly from us by sending in coupon below.